Reinvention Island

How Guernsey transformed its economy

seven times in the past 500 years

Andrew Doyle

BLUE ORMER

Copyright © 2024 Andrew Doyle.

Published by Blue Ormer Publishing.
www.blueormer.gg

Cover design and illustration by Two Degrees North.

Printed by Short Run Press, Exeter.

The right of Andrew Doyle to be identified as the author of this work has been asserted in accordance with the Copyright (Bailiwick of Guernsey) Ordinance, 2005.

All rights reserved. No part of this book may be reproduced in any form or by any means without the written permission of the publishers.

ISBN 978-1-915786-13-5

*Dedicated to my late wife Maggie and son Nolan,
and also to my very much alive daughter Amy,
who has provided encouragement throughout
the writing of this book.
And to my parents who made me curious.*

Contents

Introduction	7
1: An Unexpected Start	11
2: The Slightly Naughty Century	30
3: The Industry That Left No Trace	56
4: Guernsey Rocks	68
5: Who Killed the Guernsey Tom?	96
6: Buckets, Spades & Windbreaks	131
7: Offshore or Offside?	163
8: And the Moral of This Story Is?	210
Appendix: Data Sources for Graphs	217
Abbreviations	219
Bibliography	220
Endnotes	228
About the Author	239
Acknowledgements	240

Introduction

Relax! This is not one of those kings and queens, parliament and politicians, laws and wars history books. It's actually a story about you and me. Ordinary people. What marketers call consumers. And how the fate of Guernsey and its economy over the past 500 years has been in the hands of regular, mostly English and French, people.

These 'consumers' wanted to buy stuff, wanted their homes and surroundings to look attractive, wanted to wear, eat and drink nice things. Guernsey was able to help them get what they wanted which permitted this tiny island to grow from a population of under 10,000 in the 15th century to the extraordinary 60,000 plus today.

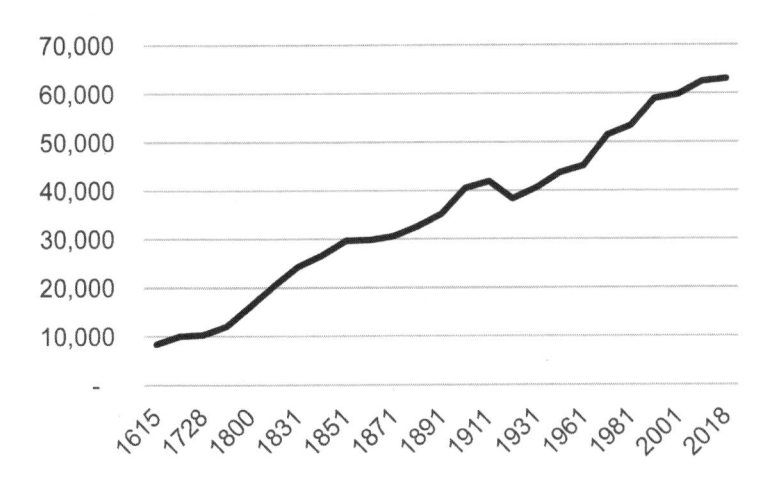

Fig 1: Population of Guernsey, 1615–2018.
(See Appendix for sources)

It's quite an amazing story and, even after writing it, I'm still astonished at the way in which this little chunk of granite in the English Channel managed to reinvent itself seven times, creating international recognition in each period for its business, and becoming, in effect, seven different trusted 'brands'. Each of these Guernsey economic iterations had slow and timid beginnings, long periods of great prosperity and then, each time, managed to screw things up by losing sight of their consumers and their brand loyalty.

It's not island laws and legislators that truly explain Guernsey's history, it's not the local landed gentry that ultimately defined the island's commercial fate, and it's not UK government interference that made the economy what it is today – it's the decisions of a multitude of ordinary households that determined this tiny island's fate.

I've got much of the information from other people's hard work and scholarship. I have stood on their shoulders to bring together in one place, this willingness of the island's population to radically change how they earn their living. You will read about some heroes and quite a few villains. There will be happy times and not so enjoyable periods. There will be unhappy endings to most of the stories but the amazing rebirths that followed will surprise you.

I also have a more personal reason for writing this book. Back in the 60s, as a teenager, I spent many years at war with my dad over the length of my hair. Every now and then, things would reach a crescendo and I would be given an ultimatum: get a haircut or leave home! So I would reluctantly walk down to St Peter Port and visit the barber in Trinity Square, just on the edge of the town centre. Near the hairdresser was a large five storey granite building. And as my coiffure was being decimated by the unsympathetic hairdresser, I used to think about this building and

INTRODUCTION

wonder what had been its purpose? Fast forward about 30 years. Sitting watching TV one evening, I came across a programme called *Who Do You Think You Are?*, which investigated each week the family history of a famous person. On this particular evening, the subject was the TV gardener, Monty Don. One of his female predecessors, many generations back, came from Dundee and was a Keiller.

Now the Keillers were, and still are, well-known Scottish manufacturers of marmalade. It turns out that in the 19th century, the UK government imposed a tax on sugar which hit Keiller's orange preserve hard and so, to avoid the potential loss of profit, the company decamped its export business to Guernsey, where this tax didn't exist and took over that large edifice, near my barbers, to house their marmalade production.[1]

This started me wondering about all the other industrial relics around the island and how they came to be there. As I travelled around the island, I began asking myself what stories were behind the strange lumps and bumps in the ground, the abandoned greenhouses, and water-filled quarries. And what about the curiously named streets and alley-ways in the islands' two towns? To use a lovely, but rarely written word, today's Guernsey in its 24.5 square miles is a palimpsest of the past – an island with many, many layers of history, there to see, if only someone would point them out.

So, let's get on and reveal the many layers that make up the stories of the seven Guernsey business brands that were created on this little wedge of rock in the English Channel, sitting in the armpit of Normandy and Brittany. Hopefully these stories will offer the people on the island today some lessons to help guide their future, as the seventh Guernsey brand: offshore finance, begins to face up to far less certain future.

The Seven Waves

~1300–1450	Subsistence
~1480–1720	Knitting
~1660–1780	Privateering/Entrepot
~1760–1860	Shipbuilding
~1780–1900	Stone Exports
~1760–2000	Tourism
~1860–1920	Tomatoes
~1920–2000	Finance

1: An Unexpected Start

At the end of the 15th century, the average Guernsey man was a farmer and fisherman. He fed his family on the crops grown on his small holding, and earned a bit of extra money selling smoked and dried mackerel and conger eel to the UK and France. This useful extra income, derived from dried and salted fish, was an important export commodity from the 13th century right up to Tudor times.

It was not an easy life, made harder by the weather, which at that time was in what has been called the little ice age. So the growing season was short, even in Guernsey. And life became even harder at the start of the 16th century.

We will talk often in this book about the positive and negative impact of government on the island, and one of the first to demonstrate this outside influence on trade was Henry VIII. In 1534, he really messed up the lucrative dried fish export business for Guernsey, with his separation from the Catholic faith. Suddenly, fish-fasting days were no longer essential. Fish eating was soon seen as 'popish flesh' by the UK population, and fish consumption started to drop. Only the conger eels were happy.

The situation was compounded by the fact that most people in the UK ate herring at that time, which was pretty tasteless when smoked or salted. So, when the discovery of the Newfoundland Grand Banks fishing area happened in the 1560s, cured and salted cod became all the rage in the UK, because it tasted so much better than either herring or Guernsey conger eel. This meant that by the mid 1500s, Guernsey fish exports were really suffering and that bit of extra money for buying essentials was disappearing.

To balance this bad news, there had also been some good news at the end of the 15th century. In 1480, the kings of England and France (Edward IV and Louis XI) agreed that the island of Guernsey should be regarded as neutral. This was confirmed in 1483, by a papal bull issued by Pope Sixtus, which meant Guernsey could trade with both France and England, even in times of war. But what could Guernsey export? How could it take advantage of this benevolent act by a far-off Pope? No one wanted its fish anymore. And the average Guernsey farmer was barely able to feed his own family, let alone have any products left over for export.

The answer was knitting, and more particularly, knitted stockings – for men! And for 200 years during the 17th and 18th centuries, Guernsey became a fashion powerhouse – a recognised and desired brand, exporting incredible amounts of carefully-knitted, colourfully-patterned, woollen stockings, initially to France and subsequently to the UK, employing up to one third of the population of the island.

This chapter is the story of the first commercial business of an island that was too small, and too heavily populated, to support itself through subsistence farming alone. And my exploration of this first fascinating foray into capitalism by Guernsey begins with some cartography.

In 1787, a wonderful map of Guernsey was unveiled. Commissioned by the Duke of Richmond and surveyed by William Gardner, it shows houses, orchards, fortifications and the incredible mosaic of fields covering the 24.5 square miles of the island.

A copy can be consulted in the Island Archives, where I was interested in reviewing the map for a later chapter on quarrying. Poring over it, I had a daft idea. I wondered how many fields there actually were on the island at that time? Having had this rash idea to count them, I sort of came to my senses, and thought perhaps a better solution would be to take three sample areas and then extrapolate from there.

1: An Unexpected Start

I took a one-mile square in the north of the island (at that time a separate entity, cut off from the rest of Guernsey by a narrow channel of sea), and similar sized squares in the parishes of St Andrew's and the Forest. All three areas turned out to have approximately 400 fields in the quadrant, and multiplying up to the 24.5 square miles of the island, I came to the incredible figure of around 10,000 fields at the end of the 18th century.

Why did I want to know this rather arcane fact about the island's topography? Well, one of Guernsey's most eminent historians, Gregory Stevens Cox, reckoned the knitting business 'arose in a Ricardian manner as a response to population pressure and land scarcity'.[1] In other words, too many people and not enough land for each family to survive comfortably – so a need to find other ways of getting income to support a household.

Why was there was too little land for effective subsistence farming? Dr Stevens Cox notes that Guernsey had an inheritance system that split the deceased's property between family members (called 'partible inheritance') with the risk of shrinking holdings – although the eldest son had the right to buy out the inheritance of his siblings. This inheritance system begins to explain the 10,000 or so fields at the end of the 18th century, with a smaller but no less difficult number at the beginning of the 17th century. Farmland for each Guernsey family was becoming smaller and smaller. By the way, a local friend told me that even today this system has its repercussions. A small piece of land he wanted to sell, turns out to belong to over 100 of his relatives spread all over the world!

Guernsey historian Rose-Marie Crossan, found an intriguing way of explaining the state of the average Guernsey farmer at the start of the 17th century.[2] She noted that in 1709, Daniel Defoe calculated it took three acres of fertile land to feed one man for a year. Now in 1615, Guernsey had between 5,000–7,000 people on the island and approximately 13,000 acres of farmable land. That means, at best, families had under three acres each, and at worst under two acres. Plus, of course not all families were equal. Some had more land than others. Or if we use my field numbers exercise, the average person had a little under one and a half fields for crop growing or animal raising.

Finally, the renowned geographer GH Dury[3] studied the 1787 map and surmised that even at the end of the 18th century, only about 50% of the island's land was under cultivation. He concluded that there was not enough to support the population adequately, given the agricultural methods employed at the time.

It's likely that in the 16th and 17th centuries, there were many families on the island who were struggling to grow enough food for themselves. They needed a new income that would allow them to pay for the food they were unable to grow themselves. And that's where knitting comes in, as it provided a source of money for the poor of the island.

Most families in Guernsey knitted for themselves at that time, but to expand into doing it commercially, they needed four things: a supply of good quality wool, money to pay for this wool, spinners and spinning wheels to create fine quality yarn, and finally a market demand.

Let's start with the money. Our Guernsey subsistence farmers certainly didn't have the cash to buy wool. As a result, we arrive for the first, but not the last time in this book, at the importance of finance in triggering an industrial innovation on the island.

Who had the money? It seems that there were 20 or so families in the island (the gentry of Guernsey: De Saumarez, Brock, Le Marchant, Dobrée and Le Mesurier, etc.) who owned large areas of land as feudal landlords and employed *rentiers* to farm for them. These estate owners were able to feed themselves and gain income from the land and the peasant farmers they employed.

Their spare money could be used for investing. And it appears that importing wool, supplying it to poor families and then buying it back as finished knitted products, was the way that our Guernsey knitting story started.

We can say that there was an economic 'push' to find extra income for both the rich and poor of the island. But there must also be a 'pull' to make the economic equation work. Who was 'pulling' the knitted stockings from the island? Who were the consumers? This is a tricky question and one which no one has really answered satisfactorily. So, let's look at it by responding to some simple questions.

Why Guernsey and knitting? Knitting was introduced into Europe by the Moors in Spain, and seems to have spread in Britain during the 14th century. Knitting with wool made a lot of sense in the UK, where much of the land was ideal for sheep. And in Guernsey it appears that sheep were widely grazed – walking along the headlands of the northern coast for example makes it an obvious area for this animal.

Wool knitting didn't need any fancy equipment and the resultant clothing was warm, light and could be made to fit the wearer.

And like most parts of Europe in the 15th century, Guernsey peasants, after a day on the land, would spend their evenings knitting clothing for their families – including that world-famous, oiled-wool fisherman's smock, the 'Guernsey'.

But why did Guernsey knitting become popular enough to create the island's first successful export business? Making clothing for your family is not an industry. That doesn't create something that would eventually employ at least one third of the population.

What triggered this change, from knitting woollen garments for your family to a vast export business in mostly stockings? We must start by understanding what people were wearing before knitted stockings became fashionable. Usually poor people wore full length 'hose' (the word that preceded stockings), made from woven cloth, using short staple wool. This material was cut to the shape of the leg using a template and then sewn together. They were baggy, available in very few colours and had little decorative pattern. They were also not very sexy! And even the rich only had velvet equivalents.

Knitted stockings, on the other hand, fitted more tightly, kept their shape longer and could be created with different colours and an infinite number of patterns. Much more comfortable and indeed sexier for the elegant male peacock – because yes, these stockings were for men, triggered by the fashion for shorter hose which emphasized their legs. On the other hand, back in the 15/16th centuries women's fashion was for dresses that reached the floor and under them were knee-length woollen socks – mainly for warmth and protection from the poor-fitting shoes they were obliged to wear.

In a wonderful article about the origins of knitted stockings in the UK, the historian Joan Thirsk describes how in 1564, a young apprentice in London spotted an Italian wearing a pair of fine wool hose made from a worsted yarn.[4] The Italian apparently lent them to the young entrepreneur who had them copied, and thus the first English worsted stockings came into being. The word 'stockings' gradually replaced 'hose' towards the end of the 16th century, with the latter being used to describe short baggy breeches.

Now you're probably wondering what this word 'worsted' means. It certainly foxed me, and so I did some investigating to discover its origins. The name comes from the Norfolk village of Worstead, which was a centre for yarn and cloth in the 12th century. Here wool was used from newly introduced breeds of sheep suited to pastures enriched through new farming techniques. Better grazing meant these new breeds produced longer wool.

'Worsted' is created using tufts from the sheep that produced long and narrow-fibred wool. The length is important because it

1: An Unexpected Start

is stronger and smoother than short-fibered curly wool from other types of sheep. But worsted not only refers to this long-fibered wool, but also to two other processes before being spun. Firstly, it was 'carded' to untangle the wool and get the fibres laying straight and secondly these fibres were then combed to remove any short ones and also help the straightening process. We'll talk more about these later.

We can imagine that the new worsted wool leggings quickly gained popularity thanks both to their practicality over cloth, and to the patterns and colours available to the fashionable man about town. As Joan Thirsk writes: 'A transformation in modes of dress had taken place. A new fashion had created a new industry'.

So how did the Channel Islands get involved in this new fashion? After all, the islands weren't noted for their sheep or wool quality. What the islands did have was a working population, with a desperate need to earn extra money to support their families. And perhaps more importantly, French-speaking local merchants, with good contacts in the fashion centres of France, and possibly some of the first wave of French Huguenots refugees following the St Bartholomew's Day Massacre in 1572, perhaps with knowledge of worsted knitted stocking techniques.

This all provided a good basis for a new island industry but there were three crucial elements, that together turned potential into reality. The first was the ability to use imported English wool and, more particularly, long staple wool from key English breeds of sheep like Border, Cotswold and Leicester. English Laws from 1614, forbade the export of wool to the continent where very little long staple wool was produced. That meant clothing produced using English wool, particularly worsted wool was highly sought-after on mainland Europe. The second element was the spinning itself. The spinning wheel is designed to twist wool fibre into thread. Worsted yarns have more twists in them than regular woollen yarn, which makes it finer, stronger and tighter. You might think, so what? The key point is that this yarn will result in a knitted product that held its shape better, was lighter and wrinkle-less – three characteristics that helped Guernsey knitted products become particularly attractive to potential buyers.

According to Thirsk, a document of 1596 reported the fine quality of Channel Islands woollen goods was achieved using special small Guernsey and Jersey spinning wheels. No one is really sure what made them so special and there are none around today to check. However, there is a spinning wheel in the Guernsey Folk Museum, which was investigated by Alan Raistrick in 2000 for the American magazine *The Spinning Wheel Sleuth*.[5] This wheel is from 1821, but is the closest we have got to the machines used in Guernsey in the 16th and 17th centuries. Mr Raistrick, when confronted with the museum spinning wheel, wrote: 'seeing it was an amazing shock' as he had expected British style equipment. It was unlike anything in the UK, and he felt it owed more to designs seen in northern France. As he wrote: 'All the Channel Islands wheels almost certainly had Picardy flyers in their time'. Flyers were used to control the number of twists that a yarn had in the spinning process.

These spinning wheels produced a yarn that was incredibly fine. In fact, so fine, so desirable, that throughout Europe the description 'Jersey' was applied to the material. What must be added though is the people who worked these spinning wheels were artisans. As Craig Muldrew notes in his article on the importance of spinning to household earnings in the period 1550–1770:

> Spinning was in fact a highly skilled occupation… This made good and reliable spinning a very marketable skill.[6]

We don't know much about the Guernsey spinners, but they were probably mostly females and often unmarried ones (hence spinsters). And if figures from 18th century British writers can be assumed to be true of Guernsey as well, then spinning was the most expensive part of converting wool to stocking yarn. Indeed, the value that merchants placed on good spinning of worsted wool, meant that up to 85% of the cost of yarn came from wages for superior spinners. This high cost explains why so much time was spent in the early 1700s creating spinning machines.

Finally, the third positive element that pushed Guernsey to create a knitting industry was the price of the imported wool itself. Wool prices had doubled from 1450 to 1550. However, after 1550, Government legislation limited wool stocks from being sold abroad, and the legislators also prevented speculators from holding on to wool with the hope of future profit. So wool prices dropped and stayed low until the beginning of the 17th century, making the import of raw material attractive for Guernsey stocking makers.

Guernsey stockings were originally for men – thigh-length individual woollen items held up with ornate garters just below the sort of long shorts or hose worn by the fashionable at that time. They were eventually replaced with joined-up leggings (around 1490) reflecting the fashion for shorter tunics.

Initially these stockings came in blue, dyed by European woad, probably imported from France or Germany. Eventually though the island exported stockings in a multitude of colours – with often one leg in one colour or pattern and the other leg in a different arrangement.

When did this industry of stocking knitting start? There were definitely indications that trade was happening in the 15th century, helped by a bit of 'scratch my back and I'll scratch yours'. It seems that in return for raising an army to help remove French invaders from the castle of Mont Orgueil in Jersey in 1468, Edward

IV granted some Guernsey merchants commercial privileges, including the right to import English raw wool at 'special rates'. This was the key trigger that underpinned the beginnings of the woollen stockings export business.

The real boom though came in the 16th century. We believe, for example, that Mary Queen of Scots wore Guernsey worsted stockings at her execution in 1578, and her sister Elizabeth paid 20 shillings for a pair of Guernsey knitted stockings embroidered with silk.

Nothing like a bit of royal patronage to create extra business. But the truth is that England was not where the Guernsey stocking merchants looked for business. Their income in the 1500s came almost entirely from France, where wool clothing lacked the quality of long worsted English yarn. The export trade to France grew and grew, reaching a zenith around the middle of the 17th century. We can identify the mid-century as a high water mark because in 1652 the Bailiff of the island presented a petition to Parliament to increase the allowance for imported wool. He noted in his petition:

> The number of inhabitants of ye said island being much increased and that ye subsistence of ye said inhabitants procedes altogether from their knitting of worsted stockings.[7]

And a little later we have a letter of Edward Dobrée, writing to Lord Hatton, asking for more wool, as follows: 'especially the Dobrees and Saumarezs they [are] trading in nothing else and employing all amongst the poor knitters of the island in relation to their Paris trade'.[8]

Wool could only be imported into the island through Southampton by Act of Parliament in 1660. And after this act, Charles II permitted the export through the Hampshire port of

1,000 tods of raw wool to the island (One tod is defined in the act as 28lbs). This was increased a little later under James II's reign to 2,000 tods (one tod is now defined as 32lbs so an allowance of 64,000lbs).

How many woollen stockings could the island and its peasant knitters make with its import of 64,000lbs of raw wool a year? Dr Stevens Cox uses a Jersey statistic from 1687, which noted that 6,000 knitters made 6,000 pairs of stockings a week and that involved 100 tods, or 3,200lbs of raw wool. By extrapolation, Stevens Cox estimates that in a year, the 2,000 tods allowance would result in 120,000 pairs of stockings being made in Guernsey, by about 3,000 people. And given estimates for the population of the island at the end of the 17th century was about 8,000[9] – these 3,000 wool spinners, carders, combers and knitters amounted to over a third of the total population.

I am always a bit cynical about taking figures from the past at face value, as you never know what lies behind them. So I started wondering if it would be possible to recreate those 16th century stockings today. Fortunately, someone else had the same idea. Mara Riley in America has a website dedicated to period dress and has made some 18th century stockings – so a bit later than our period. She reckoned that such a pair would use 'about 8 to 14oz of wool yarn, depending on gauge and the size of the stockings'.[10] Now going back to the Stevens Cox calculations, the 120,000 pairs of stockings would work out at 8.5oz each, so quite compatible with the practical work of Mara Riley.

There are still a couple of things that are a bit worrying about all these estimates. First, the Guernsey knitters didn't just produce stockings, they produced many other items of clothing. In 1611, Heylyn wrote:

'The principall commodity which they use to send abroad are the works and labours of the poorer sort as waste-cotes, stockins and other manufactures made of wool.'[11]

So, the likelihood is that the 2,000 tod license was used to make more than just stockings.

Whatever the answer, just having the capacity to make lots of stockings a year doesn't necessarily guarantee business. That required salesmanship, retail outlets and attractiveness for potential consumers. So how did the stocking business work back in the 17th century?

It started with island entrepreneurs (the landed gentry) who obtained licenses from the island's Governor or his representative, for the importation of a fixed quantity of uncombed wool (within the total allowance for the island). People like the de Saumarez family would use their license to buy in the raw wool from the UK. Some even sent representatives to live in places like Southampton, Lyme and Poole to supervise wool imports. Checking on what was bought was vital as it was only long staple wool with its narrow fibres that could produce the quality expected by customers.

They then sold this raw wool on to a Guernsey carder or comber who would wash, comb, dye and get the wool spun into yarn by accomplished spinners. They would in turn sell the yarn on to a merchant who would put it out to knitters, telling them what style, colours and patterns to follow, based on the demands of their customers in France. To ensure an acceptable quality, the merchants would get the knitters to work in large rooms or 'boutiques' where they could be more easily managed. They could be apparently rather lively sessions. In 1667, an ordinance of the Royal Court dealt with the 'unruly behaviour of women, girls and boys who assembled in boutiques and chambres to knit stockings'.[12]

1: An Unexpected Start

This rather convoluted system of wool importers, carders, combers, spinners, dyers and knitters, reflected the reality that no one in the island had enough money to underwrite the whole operation.

It seems that on average a knitter could produce roughly one to two pairs of stockings a week and received cash based on a piece rate price. We know from contemporary letters that for example, the wife of Matthew de Saumarez, Bertranne, would handle the knitters and supervise their work, resulting in her receiving around 40 pairs of what were called *bas à canon* stockings each week from her outworkers. The finished stockings would then be taken by another family member, Michael, and sold in France.

It's fair to ask the question: why would French people buy Guernsey stockings when the country had its own knitters? It seems that English wool had a strong positive brand image abroad – not just in France, but as far afield as Venice and Hungary. And it helped that James I, in the early 1600s, had banned the export of English wool outside Great Britain – Guernsey was considered part of Great Britain, and if you remember, the island's neutrality meant it could legitimately trade with France.

The quality of the wool, its spinning, and the expertise of Guernsey knitters in creating ultra-fine textures (ten stitches per inch) for the wool products, meant that their products were particularly highly prized. As Heylyn notes in 1629, the locals were 'exceedingly cunning at their craft'.[13]

And Charles Trumbull in his journal of 1677 notes:

The stockings are generally of a finer sort than those of Jersey, some of them so curiously knit and so fine that they may be drawn through a ring and worth 20/– or 30/–.[14]

The strong ties between the island and France through language and proximity, meant that the local merchants were able to get up-to-date information on the latest French fashions. This information could then be used to direct the work of the local knitters, who were able to supply stockings in up to 50 different colours with names like 'Amorous Desire', 'Resuscitation Corpse' and 'Dying Spaniard'.

Bas à canon stockings were particularly fashionable in the 17th century. These were tight around the calf but then widening below the knee and tucked in over boots. Colours and patterns varied enormously with many different varieties mentioned in local correspondence. Not only eye-catching but, as we said earlier, Guernsey stockings didn't wrinkle and kept their shape, thanks to the worsted yarn.

These *bas à canon* stockings were sold for between 5 and 10 shillings a pair at the end of the 17th century. Not cheap when you consider the cost of a return fare to St Malo at the time was only 4 shillings.

There are many contemporary references to how important the knitting industry was to the island. In 1643, the Earl of Warwick wrote: 'wool imployed by the poore inhabitants to the making of stockings, which is the onlie meanes that they have to get their living'.[15]

And in 1677, Charles Trumbull described St Peter Port as inhabited by 'Stocking merchants as they will call themselves, those that buy all the stockings that are made in the island and barter or sell them away by wholesale to France'.[16]

Guernsey artisans weren't the only people knitting stockings in the 17th century. All over the UK, farming communities were beavering away, knitting mostly stockings for export. According to official export figures, by the end of the 17th century, the UK was exporting between 1,000,000 and 1,750,000 pairs of woollen stockings.[17] This meant the tiny island of Guernsey was responsible for a market share of between 10 and 20% of the whole UK export business to the rest of Europe (mainly Ireland, France and Holland). And it is highly likely that this market share was a lot higher in the early years of the century, when Guernsey was at the forefront of the trend in knitted worsted stockings. Indeed, the two Channel Islands were so innovative with their knitting that French agents were dispatched there to learn how they achieved their quality.

We shouldn't be surprised that Guernsey achieved success in France. They spoke the same language, there were many family ties and St Peter Port was a familiar trading port for the French. Contemporary reports also noted the French trusted Guernsey merchants, whilst being less certain about those from England. These cultural benefits must have helped Guernsey market its stockings at the expense of English equivalents.

The huge growth of exported stockings took some knocks in the second half of the 17th century – first by the Civil War in the England, and then by a series of problems in France. It seems that the Guernsey knitters got a bit sloppy with their work and we have letters of complaint to the island from their representatives in France. Apparently, Guernsey-knitted goods 'did not merit the reputation for excellence that they had enjoyed under the Tudors'.[18]

This lackadaisical quality, plus the high cost of spinners, probably helped the growth of knitting machines in France (developed as a result of industrial espionage – stealing blueprints and even actual machines from the UK).

Finally, the French government got involved and banned the importation of stockings in 1668. This action reflected the protectionist policy of the French finance minister, Colbert, who successfully nurtured many manufacturing start-ups in France, including machine knitting, designed to meet increased French demand for woollen clothing, including stockings. Indeed, the lower cost of machine-made stockings hit the more artisanal Guernsey variety hard. In 1684, William Le Marchant in Paris concluded: 'What prevents one selling them is that they are extremely dear'.[19]

The French actions, combined with England's William III in 1689, ending Guernsey's commercial neutrality and prohibiting the sale of wool products to the enemy France. This led to a period of stagnation in Guernsey and the loss of export income triggered local merchants to turn their attention to the UK mainland, and fairly quickly, business grew again.

As early as 1699, nearly 3,000 pairs of Guernsey stockings were exported to the UK. In fact, the first half of the 18th century was boom time again for stockings from Guernsey. A small group of merchants purchased the raw wool import licenses and engaged a very large number of knitters on the island; some historians putting it as much as a quarter of the population. Estimates for this period suggest that hand knitted woollen stockings accounted for almost half the value of all exports from the island to the UK.

In fact, the export to the UK of stockings was pretty stable throughout most of the 18th century – historian Richard Hocart trawled through the National Archives and was able to identify annual UK imports from Guernsey with numbers varying from just under 24,000 pairs, to as much as 168,000 in 1750, with a century average of 45,600 pairs a year.[20]

What is remarkable with these figures is that Guernsey-made stockings had not only to cover the costs of wool, the carding and dyeing, spinning into yarn and then knitting into stockings – it also bore the cost of transport from Southampton of the raw wool and the shipping of finished products back to the UK. In theory competitors on the mainland did not face this added cost.

The key word here is 'in theory'. In reality, the awful quality of the roads in 18th century Britain meant that transportation by sea was quicker and cheaper than movement on land. In Peter Johnson's book *A Short History of Guernsey*, the author claims it took nearly two days, over land, to get from St Peter Port to Pleinmont at the far west of the island – a distance of under eight miles!

Guernsey's refocus on the export of stockings to the UK in the 18th century had another benefit. London, one of the world's biggest cities at the time was only a 40-hour sail from St Peter Port. And what did London have lots of? Middle-class people. People with money to spare. People with an eye to fashion. People who wanted to wear fashionable stockings – and have clean ones on a regular basis. 'Clean ones' is perhaps a misnomer, as most people made do with just two pairs a year! We can imagine a lot of the 45,000 pairs of stockings exported from Guernsey each year ended up in the middle-class homes of professional people in London and other urban ports around the country.

Hocart's figures, showing this average of 45,000 pairs of stockings produced a year, is by no means the maximum that the island could produce. Remember the king had agreed to allow the island to import 2,000 tods of wool a year? Well, throughout the 18th century, Guernsey averaged an import figure of only 1,175 tods a year – just over half the permitted allowance. In 1771, William Le Marchant wrote: 'We do not so much as import two-thirds of the 2000 tods yearly allowed us from England'.[21] It is probable that there was also smuggled wool that got into the island.

From a high point in 1750, stocking exports showed an inexorable downward curve, with a low point of 12,000 pairs in 1780. Why this decline? Many historians point the finger at Lancashire and the booming mills of the industrial revolution, resulting in the churning out of cheap cotton that could be turned into stockings to undercut the island's wool versions.

There were other reasons. Once the French government had made the lucrative sale of Guernsey stockings much more difficult, those knitters found themselves competing with their UK equivalents and, although shipping from the island was cheaper and quicker than road transport for the stocking makers of East Anglia and the Midlands, nevertheless, St Peter Port merchants found it necessary to reduce the pay of their outworkers. Many of the 3,000 or so knitters on the island found themselves working for pennies. And so, they began to look around for other means of employment.

My favourite reason for the decline of Guernsey stockings is Beau Brummel. This famous early 19th century toff single-handedly brought about the decline of men as fashion peacocks as he introduced the idea of the dark suit. He started wearing full length, very tight trousers, and his fame in London meant that, pretty quickly, men started copying him. Long trousers meant no need for stockings.

Did the decline in stocking knitting result from a push by the industrial revolution, the impact of Beau Brummel, or were our locals pulled by the attraction of alternative means of employment? There is a good argument for putting the blame less on the dark satanic mills of Manchester and Leeds, or the persuasiveness of Beau Brummel, and more on the seductive power and wages of three alternative industries that we will cover in the next chapter.

Whatever the cause of the decline in stocking exports, by 1830 John Jacobs wrote that 'this handicraft trade is almost, if not entirely, lost'.[22] And an industry that had been the toast of Europe, that had sustained the rural population and employed a large percentage of the island population, died.

1: An Unexpected Start

Well, almost died. The first island industry is still remembered today in many parts of the world thanks to the continuing survival of the 'Guernsey'. This unique relic of the Tudor fisherman's uniform is still made on the island today. Still using that complex and distinctive pattern. Still made with water-resistant worsted wool. Still mostly in that well known blue. A tangible reminder of a time when the Guernsey brand was at the epicentre of a fashion industry that employed thousands of local people.

So, what did all those spinners, dyers and knitters on the island find that was so much more lucrative than making stockings? Absolutely nothing to do with clothing – as you are about to find out.

2: The Slightly Naughty Century

We could describe the 16th and 17th centuries in Guernsey as the adolescent years of the island's economy. In these centuries, both high and low-born Guernsey men and women learned the realities of business, rode the crest of a fashion boom, overcame French legislative nastiness, developed a woollen brand with a high reputation, and created a lot of capital, which sloshed around the coffers of the local merchant gentry.

Now we arrive at the 18th century and what we might call the early adulthood of Guernsey commerce or, maybe better, the slightly naughty century. Naughty because two of the four industries, that bit by bit replaced knitting were sort of dodgy. We are talking here about privateering and smuggling. The third, the St Peter Port entrepôt era, was their more reputable offspring. The fourth, quarrying, which was also much more ethical, will have its own chapter later.

The St Peter Port Entrepôt

All four industries had one thing in common. They were dependent on the sea – as bringer of materials and as transporter of finished goods. And what we need to remember is that the 18th century was not a good time for road transport. In fact, it was a ghastly time for getting from A to B on land. The roads were a joke – poorly maintained, unlit with lousy surfaces, frequently under water, open to ambush from highway men. Anywhere took an eternity to get to.

Now contrast all this with the sea and ships. Even before steam, sail and wind provided pretty rapid propulsion, with most towns

2: THE SLIGHTLY NAUGHTY CENTURY

and cities situated on water and so, accessible. And there was Guernsey, deep water just off St Peter Port, a protected harbour, repair yards, access to professional shipbuilders, rope makers, blacksmiths and handy cool cellars for warehousing, plus shops, inns, hostels, brothels, fresh water, and good cider.

So don't look on Guernsey 300 years ago as a backwater, but rather as an extremely handy, heavily used, prototype motorway service station, with access to quick routes for England and France, as well as the start of long-distance seaways to the Americas and the Far East. A sort of Watford Gap of its day!

I'd like you to imagine Guernsey's main town of St Peter Port, say around 1678. If you know today's elegant bustling centre, that 17th century version looked very different. No winding road at its southern extremity, up the Val des Terres. No road along the front by Havelet Bay, just a steep shingled beach. No multiple marinas, just one three-sided granite-walled harbour, stretching from the Town Church to the Pier Steps, protected by Castle Cornet, isolated on its rocky island.

The Town Church was there, with three streets radiating out from it in southerly, northerly and westerly directions. Clinging to these thoroughfares were very tall, gabled, timber-clad, thatched-roof houses that petered out quickly to the south and west, but straggled on north, to the Salerie Corner, where they lost the will to go any further. The tiny centre was crowded, dirty and smelly, with dribbles of wastewater snaking down the streets' central gulleys.

But don't imagine it was a gloomy, sleepy town. It was a buzzy place, home to about one third of the island's population. Full of horses and carts, picking up bales of wool from Southampton ships, or dropping off stockings and waistcoats to be taken aboard French ships bound for the ports of Brittany and Normandy. The same ships that delivered produce from those two fertile departments, plus wines from further south. And now and then, sailing vessels docking to take on board the rounded stones from the northern parish bays, destined to become the solid streets of Portsmouth, Winchester and other Hampshire towns. Buildings full of merchants negotiating, spinners spinning, knitters knitting, dyers dyeing, combers and carders straightening wool, sail makers repairing, sailors carousing, as well as a market full of butchers, fishmongers, greengrocers and bakers supporting the town's people.

To sum it up, St Peter Port became what they call an *entrepôt*, a word often used to describe Guernsey's main town in the 18th century. But what does this mean? Wikipedia gives a pretty good definition: 'An entrepôt or transhipment port is a port, city, or trading post where merchandise may be imported, stored, or traded, usually to be exported again'.[1]

My earlier description of St Peter Port as a sort of motorway service station for the sailing ship era is also pretty good. It was a place to stop en route to somewhere else.

What triggered the creation of this entrepôt? It all started with that famous granting of neutrality to the island in 1483 by Pope Sixtus IV. Everyone was welcome to trade in the island, even if they were at war with England. Then there is the geography of St Peter Port. It was handy for ships from Holland, France and Scandinavia, heading south to Africa, and it was convenient for ships going west across the Atlantic to either the West Indies or America. It was also well placed for ships returning from either of these directions.

Why would they want to stop here? Just like a motorway service station, many of these ships found it a good place to anchor for the night, have something to eat or drink, before carrying on with their journey. But this is almost to trivialise St Peter Port as an attractive place to stop.

2: THE SLIGHTLY NAUGHTY CENTURY

What really made the town special was its focus on making life easy to conduct business. That doesn't sound a big deal, does it? But at the end of the 17th century, governments of the big European nations were all adopting an economic policy called mercantilism. This meant that each country tried to maximise its exports and minimise its imports. High tariffs were put on imported goods to discourage them, and colonies were only allowed to trade with the mother country.

This was not much fun for commercial organisations who did not like being told with whom they could or could not trade. And that's where St Peter Port was able to play a role. As a neutral, it was outside the high tariff walls of European countries. It saw itself as a friend to all and an enemy to none.

The stocking business led the way. Those ships bringing wool from Southampton to the island needed to be serviced. They had sails to be repaired, crews to be fed and entertained, return trip supplies to be provided. And then there were the sailing vessels taking finished stockings to France or further afield. They arrived with cargo to be sold – wine, tobacco, produce from the farms of France. The Guernsey merchants were keen to acquire and sell on these items. So, for example, around the town, local entrepreneurs excavated approximately 20–30 cellars to hold and mature big quantities of wines and spirits or store tobacco.

Both the alcohol and tobacco warehousing required more than just a suitable storage facility. The big ships from France arrived with claret and cognac in bulk – in wooden barrels or hogsheads, holding around 300 litres. This made them often ungainly for further shipment in smaller quantities. The same was true for tobacco which arrived in large wooden barrels that held around 454 kilos of product.

Some wine and spirit owners could not afford to bring their full cargo straight into England, as they would be required to pay full duty on it. As there was no duty in Guernsey, they could store their goods in local cellars and ship small quantities back to England when they had the money to pay the tax. Then there were others who had no intention of paying tax in England. They needed to breakdown their wares into smaller units, which would be easier to sell in compact quantities to buyers who could sneak them ashore in France or the UK.

This story applies equally to tobacco, dropped off by ships coming from the New World but also from the UK. Guernsey was an important source of this commodity for France, where the creation in 1674 of a tobacco royal monopoly (and obligatory tax) made smuggling very attractive. Stevens Cox quotes Professor Jacob Price who calculated that Guernsey imported from England, several hundred thousand pounds in weight of tobacco a year, which ended up being quietly moved to France by French smugglers.

There was clearly a need to break down the cargoes into more handy units. This led to a boom in coopers who created more appropriately sized containers – either 'dry' barrels for tobacco or 'wet' for alcohol. According to Stevens Cox, 'by the early nineteenth century there were some seven hundred coopers working in the St Peter Port entrepôt'.[2] These were skilled workers, and we will see their influence later when we describe the island's next economic revolution.

We can see how the creation of the St Peter Port entrepôt came about through a number of influences. The geographic location of town which attracted shipping. A well protected harbour. The cellars carved into the steep slope above this harbour for holding and bulk-breaking wines, spirits and tobacco. And a large cohort of well-trained coopers to create easy-to-handle barrels both for wet and dry products.

It all comes together into something even bigger. St Peter Port became a sort of Aladdin's cave for merchants throughout Europe.

2: The Slightly Naughty Century

A place where you could buy or sell just about anything. A place with no eagle-eyed customs officers. A place where the French felt at home thanks to the French speaking population. A place of free trade. A place where the restricting mercantile policies of France and England did not apply. A place for both the law-abiding and the law-evading.

It must have been an incredibly lively place. Full of activity. Filled with the voices of many nations. No wonder it attracted people from Guernsey's rural parishes, whose income from knitting was dwindling. In St Peter Port they could be labourers in warehouses or help build the many elegant multi-storeyed houses being thrown up for the rich locals. They could serve in these houses, or work for one of the 60 plus *marchants et negociants*. They could also learn how to be a cooper or join one of the burgeoning armadas of Guernsey-based ships needing crews (around 77 in 1789).

In 1787, the Bailiff of Guernsey mused that without the explosion in commerce in St Peter Port, two-thirds of the island population would have needed to emigrate (quoted by Stevens Cox). Instead, the wealth of the entrepôt led to a veritable explosion in house re-fronting or building, and led to the creation of the elegant town of St Peter Port that we see today.

But there were black clouds on the horizon at the end of the 17th century. In 1678, there were more than a few merchants discussing, with local feudal landowners, the ending by William III of the neutrality of the island. Worrying that their friends, relatives and clients on the French mainland were now their enemies. What would happen to all their knitting business? Where would their income come from in the future? Would the French attack the island, would the defences be enough?

Even though the islanders spoke the same language and shared common ancestry, they were spooked at the thought of an invasion by their powerful Gallic next-door neighbour. As the *Morning Chronicle* noted in September 1778 during the American War of Independence: 'The intention of the French to land in Guernsey and Jersey is absolute fact'.[3]

There was probably also a 'whoops!' moment within the UK government, as they saw how their cancellation of neutrality could lead to unforeseen consequences. What would happen if the French decided to invade the Channel Islands? They realised that their booming global mercantile business, which often ended up in riches-laden ships going through the narrow straits of the English Channel (already back then the busiest sea lane in the world), could be exposed to a potentially hostile French-owned Channel Islands at one end and the already fearfully aggressive Dunkirk privateers at the other. An east and west 'Dunkirk' was a frightening thought.

And just back to stockings for one moment, our Guernsey merchants who paid for imported wool and underwrote the export of finished knitted goods, were also panicked by the potential for attacks on their cargoes from French naval vessels, now they were no longer protected by neutrality. So, they were desperate to safeguard their watery links with the mainland.

Many people with a lot to lose. What to do? The British government knew it could not afford the cost of protecting all its global assets and sea lanes with its own Navy. It had to supplement it, sub-contract it if you like, to outside help. And this was the idea behind privateers – the first of the two slightly dodgy industries that eventually replaced knitting. Two industries that kept our St Peter Port entrepôt bustling and successful for more than 100 years.

2: The Slightly Naughty Century

Privateering

Privateers were armed ships, privately equipped, granted the right by governments to attack the enemy and take its cargo as booty – shared initially between the Crown, the ship owners and the crew. The privateer got these rights through the issuing of what was called a *Letter of Marque*, which said in a very legalese way: 'Look, we know you were attacked by the enemy, so here is a document, which legally entitles you to retribution for your losses'. The letter was issued to the captain of the privateer and had all sorts of rules that had to be followed, including the split of any profits – a fifth to the Crown, two-thirds of the rest to the ship owners, and the remaining third to the poor crew who had to take all the risks fighting the enemy.

So, privateers were not pirates. Well, most of the time they weren't. As you can imagine, Guernsey's French-speaking crews were not averse on occasions to pretending they were French privateers in order to attack British cargo ships. And privateers were not unique to Great Britain. The French and many others had similar set-ups and as noted earlier, the privateers of Dunkirk were particularly feared.

They were therefore seen as protectors of sea lanes and trade links, defenders of Guernsey sovereignty, disrupters of foreign trade competitors and, lastly, a very interesting, potentially lucrative, investment by island merchants and capital holders.

When Did Privateers Operate?

There were already privateers in the reign of Elizabeth I, but most Guernsey privateering took place between 1692 (the Battle of La Hogue) and the end of the Napoleonic Wars (1815). During this period of just over 100 years, the main actions occurred during the many wars between England and France – the War of the Great Alliance (1688–1697), the War of Spanish Succession (1701–1714), the War of Austrian Succession (1740–1748), the Seven Years' War (1756–1763), the American War of Independence (1777–1783), the French Revolutionary War (1792–1802) and the Napoleonic Wars (1803–1815). In other words, just about two thirds of the 18th century!

The Costs of Privateering

We noted at the start of this chapter that there was a 'push' towards privateering from the cash-limited UK Government, who wanted help protecting the sea lanes around the English Channel. But also from the Guernsey people who wanted to avoid being overrun by the French. It was all very well wanting this, but somebody actually had to do the privateering. And pay for it. So, we need to investigate the 'pull' of this activity. And head of the queue were the merchants of the island. They had thousands of local people knitting woollen garments for them that were destined for the UK, and they didn't relish the danger of French ships attacking Guernsey vessels, loaded with stockings, on their way to the mainland. Clearly, they needed armed ships to ward off the French. A good example of these merchants was Monsieur de St George Jean Guille, whose life and times has been described by local historian Richard Hocart. Monsieur de St George was part of the gentry of Guernsey, but that didn't mean his life was one of genteel decadency. Hocart points out that this gentleman 'invested in and managed privateers'.[4]

The merchants from Guernsey and the mainland saw another benefit of privateering. The end of the 17th century experienced a significant growth in the middle classes in the UK, and allied to this growth, a boom in consumerism. People started buying stuff because they wanted to, rather than because they had to. That's why the riches of the colonies around the world were being harvested by the colonial powers. There was a significant market for things like spices, silks, furs, tea and coffee.

At the start of each of the wars identified above, there were many richly-laden French merchant ships, returning to France from the colonies, or sailing along the coast with wine from Bordeaux. These were now potentially fair game for Guernsey privateers, and more importantly, attractive wins for merchant investors. The pull of this potentially rich return encouraged local merchants to stump up the money for privateering ships.

What were the costs involved? First of all, the ships themselves. These were either existing merchant ships that were converted, or ships built and purchased in the UK (usually in the southwest of England). Yes, there were a few built in Guernsey, but they were the minority. And the ships purchased in England were apparently mainly of French origin (captured by the British). It seems that the Channel Islands fleet of converted ships was the only European privateering centre that did not build their own boats.

Now we are not talking about big ships here. Most Guernsey privateers, according to Jamieson's *A People of the Sea* were around 60 tons (about the same size as the *Speedwell*, the Pilgrim Fathers' second ship), compared to British vessels at the time of 200 tons or more.[5] Apparently there were even Guernsey rowing boats armed with a single gun and twenty or so blood-thirsty sailors. According to a study in 1986 by Canon Peter Raban, it cost 'between £13 and £15 per ton to convert, equip, arm and crew a privateer for its first cruise'.[6]

Now I don't know about you, but quoting historic money amounts doesn't really help me. I know it's what historians must do for accuracy, but I wanted to get a feel for the real value. So, I have used two methods to help. The Bank of England has a section in its website called the Inflation Calculator, which translates money from any given period in history to its equivalent today. And a second, the American website, measuringworth.com, which does the same using a Retail Price Index.

The Bank of England's inflation calculator suggests that an English pound in 1700, would be the equivalent of £200 today, whilst the measuringworth.com site suggests it would be worth £147.50. That means to prepare for its first cruise, a ready-built 60-ton privateer with around eight guns and 60 crew, would have cost investors between £124,000 and £170,000 in today's money.

What did they get for their investment? Our estimate above assumes that the boat already exists, so the money covered the conversion from a peace-time vessel to an armed aggressor, the equipping of it with weapons and the hiring of crew plus their food and drink for around two months.

Who Invested in Privateers?

We mentioned earlier about the need by Guernsey merchants to safeguard the sea lanes to the mainland, plus their commercial interest in the benefit of plundering French merchantmen. So, it's not surprising to learn that local Guernsey merchants were the main investors in privateers. And according to Jamieson's *A People of the Sea*, there were 35 key people who effectively bankrolled the privateering century – the big local merchants like the Dobrées, the de Saumarezs, the Le Marchants, the Priaulxs and the Maingys.[7]

During the first period of privateering (the wars of the Great Alliance and the Spanish Succession), a lot of Guernsey people dabbled in privateer ship investment. It was a new kind of lottery for them, inspired by the hype about potential winnings, which meant that in this first flush of privateering, ships often had six or more owners. And investors put money into more than one ship. Below are some examples recorded in the Guernsey Letters of Marque:

> In 1708 Joseph Chubb was the master of the privateer galley the *Guernsey*, owned by 'Peter Stephens, Nicholas Lobelly [Le Pelley], Thomas le Marchant, Nicholas Carey, Michael Falla and Widow Poundwell, all of Guernsey,' and the galley *Prince Eugene*, sent out by 'John Saumares, François Martin, Peter de la Place and Joseph la Falle of Guernsey' and by 'Saumerye, Lawrence Martin and John Lewis of Guernsey, merchants.[8]

The smaller investors were quickly put off further involvement, once they saw that their privateer ships could be unsuccessful, captured, ransomed or sunk (30% of privateers in the War of Spanish Succession took no prizes and up to 40% were sunk). And for the rest of the century the bigger merchants dominated investments.

How Many Guernsey Privateers were Involved?

To be honest the number of Guernsey ships involved in privateering is a bit of a muddle, when you examine the history books. There is confusion between Letters of Marque issued to ship's captains, and identification of active ships during the 18th century. *Donkipedia*[9] is really helpful for the first half of the 18th century, so here is what I reckon the fleet looked like in the era of privateering.

We can start by noting that in 1697, 30 Guernsey privateers existed, which rose to 105 vessels during the War of Spanish Succession (1701–1714). Then there is a figure of 43 ships at the start of the War of Austrian Succession (1740–1748) and 121 vessels during the Seven Years' War (1756–1763). There were approximately 90 Guernsey privateers during the American War of Independence, about 100 during the French Revolution, and around 35 more in 1800. Overall, it appears there was an average of nearly 100 Guernsey ships of various sizes operating as privateers during most of the 18th century.

Again, using *Donkipedia*, we can get an idea of the size of the privateers. At the start of the 18th century, during the War of Spanish Succession, the average size was 55 tons. This rose to 62 tons during the War of Austrian Succession, and 89 tones during the Seven Years War – perhaps rising to around 100 tons by the Napoleonic wars.

These tonnages are hard to imagine. After a bit of searching online, I found the dimensions of a Royal Navy cutter built in 1763, called HMS *Fly*.[10] This weighed 78 tons and was 14 metres long and 6 metres wide – roughly four Fiat 500s or a London double decker bus in length and three London bus widths.

How Did Privateers Operate?

As noted earlier, the privateering adventure started with an investment by one or more merchants. They hired a captain, who had a Letter of Marque, allowing him to seek retribution for 'losses' caused by enemy ships. The investment funds were used to either build or transform a merchant vessel into a warship, acquire a crew and fill the ship with provisions for up to a five-month voyage.

These voyages would take place in the calmer seas of spring and summer. Most Guernsey ships looked for prizes to the west of St Brieuc in Brittany and down the coast to Bordeaux. These were waters they knew very well, and sometimes Guernsey ships were even used by English privateers as pilots. Guernsey privateers were particularly good at hiding behind the little rocky islets that litter the seas between the Channel Islands and the west coast of France, ambushing merchantmen as they went by. They also used sea mists and early morning or night attacks to surprise the enemies. And thanks to their shallow draught, bigger ships could not pursue them in these tricky waters. Apparently, the Guernsey privateers were also adept at sneaking into harbours and taking foreign ships at anchor.

I love this example from the *Gentleman's Magazine* of 1832, quoting a story from the start of the American War of Independence:

> Little bands of neighbours putting their few hundred pounds together, subscribed sufficient to purchase a lugger, to be fitted out as a privateer. The orders were dispatched to Peter Perchard. Mangles, the ship-chandler, furnished for him. The guns were had from the Carron Company.
>
> All ready, and a crew of resolute fellows not to be baffled, and knowing every inch of the French coast, and valuing life hardly at a pin's fee, commanded by a man, too, speaking French usually better than English; silent and dark as the night, out warped these low but well found boats, and the French West Indiamen were the game they chiefly ran down. They lay low in the water, and every shot they fired into vessels heavily laden took effect. They boarded the enemy usually with little loss of life or limb, and in a few weeks we had the papers of the prize transmitted, to apply for her condemnation in the Admiralty Court.[11]

Back at the start of the 18th century when privateering was fairly new to Guernseymen, they would aim to capture enemy vessels in short 30-minute battles, clap the captured foreign sailors in irons and put their own crew (about half a dozen men) on the ship, and sail it back to either Guernsey or to a UK port. This partly explains why the early Channel Island privateers had such large crews (roughly one crew member per ton) – they needed to allow for losing a proportion to crew captured ships. These large numbers also reflected the style of those early battles which were less about broadsides of cannon fire and more about hand-to-hand combat. So, the bigger the crew, the better were your chances of success.

Later in the century, it became obvious to the merchants underwriting the ventures that huge crews were costly, and selling off captured vessels time-consuming. So very cleverly, later in the 18th century, Guernsey privateers switched to ransoming the foreign vessels they captured. Here is an example quoted in the *Gentleman's Magazine* in 1748: 'April 1748. A prize, with wine and brandy, and a ransomer of £1000, taken by the Hanover privateer of Guernsey'.[12]

Ransoming became something of a speciality for Guernsey privateers. They would capture the foreign vessel and then demand a ransom from the owner, sometimes letting the captured ship sail away whilst retaining crew members as hostages until the ransom had been paid. For example, during the War of Spanish Succession, of the 746 boats captured by Guernsey privateers, 172 of them were ransomed.

The Financial Benefits of Privateering

Lots of privateers, lots of ships, lots of investors. But did the investment produce a return? The following figures emerge from various documents, in values of the times, plus, in brackets, today's rate, using both the Bank of England inflation index and the website measuringworth.com:

- War of Spanish Succession: £200,000 (£28–£38 million)
- The Seven Years War: £900,000 (£128–£175 million)

- The US War of Independence: £2,000,000 (£236–£296 million)

Today's values can only be indicative, but it just shows that privateering was a worthwhile investment for some Guernsey merchants. To qualify this further, it has been noted that the value of Guernsey seizures during the War of Spanish Succession was more than the numbers taken by the whole of the British Navy. Guernsey was good at this privateering business! Of course, not everyone made money by investing in privateers. Some ships captured nothing, some were themselves taken and others were sunk.

What Happened to the Captured Prizes?

Some interesting sums of money were won during the various 18th century wars. But this money wasn't sitting in treasure chests on board captured foreign vessels. What was resting in the holds of these ships were cargoes that varied according to their port of origin. We noted earlier that Guernsey privateers specialised in attacking coastal shipping along the French mainland of Brittany down to Bordeaux. This meant lots of wine, brandy, agricultural goods, and construction materials. Guernsey boats also occasionally ran across French ships going to, or coming from the West Indies, full of spices, spirits, molasses and tobacco.

The captured cargoes would have either been taken to the UK to be 'condemned' by the British authorities and then sold at auction, or more often than not, sailed to St Peter Port, thus avoiding UK taxes on the plunder. Either way, merchants would come from all over the continent and UK to buy what was on offer. These merchants would then take their purchases and find customers for them. Sometimes these were thoroughly legitimate transactions, but there were also more dubious activities — smugglers who bought the merchandise and would then sneak them into the UK to avoid customs duties.

How Big was the Guernsey Privateering Industry?

Edmund Burke remarked in Parliament that the Channel Islands privateer fleet could almost be entitled to be called: 'one of the naval powers of the world'.[13] And at the end of the 18th century, it can be estimated that Guernsey had around 125 privateers, and employed a total crew of probably over 3,000 men and boys, of which at least a half were Guernsey-born. So, let's say around 1,500 Guernsey males were crew on the ships in 1800. That's around 10% of the total island population. But of course, privateers don't set sail without a huge 'back office' staff. You have to provide food and drink for the crews, the ship's sails need repairing, ropes need to be replaced, hulls need to be patched and made watertight. Ammunition needed to be supplied, and armaments replaced, repaired or updated. Small arms would be provided, and swords sharpened. The list is pretty long. It would be quite reasonable to guess that 25% of the population of the island in 1800 would one way or another be employed in the privateering business.

The importance of the servicing of the privateers can for example, be confirmed by the Royal Court being informed in 1748 that catering the privateer fleet 'was placing a strain on the supply of meat for islanders'.[14] And let's not forget about other ancillary service functions stimulated by the privateers. Half the sailors came from outside the island, and so needed lodgings before setting sail. They needed feeding and it's probable they also drank heavily and used prostitutes. So, our figure of 25% of the population is not at all unrealistic. It was big business. And we can imagine it helped create a solution in employment for all those wool knitters who,

2: THE SLIGHTLY NAUGHTY CENTURY

as the 18th century progressed, found themselves increasingly working for peanuts. The many opportunities for employment created by privateers would have been a better-paid alternative.

It is worth pausing here to consider the hidden results of privateering. First of all, once the original idea of giving part of the booty to the reigning monarch had not surprisingly been kicked out, privateering became quite a democratic business. Like piracy, each crew member shared in the riches they obtained. Quite different from the Royal Navy at the time, where getting paid was often very difficult and where the conditions were absolutely not democratic. No wonder the Guernsey privateers found it easy recruiting ex-Royal Navy sailors. At the end of the War of Spanish Succession in 1716, the author Sam Allende reckoned two-thirds of the sailors in the Royal Navy were made redundant. Well-trained, thoroughly professional, and in possession of many skills, these men had no difficulty finding employment on privateers.

Secondly, privateering was, in effect, officially condoned robbery. So, each time a war ended during the 18th century, privateers simply exchanged the Red Ensign for the Jolly Roger and became pirates. When another war started, the pirates would move back into privateering. And so there took place a sort of ping-pong match in the 18th century – with Guernsey vessels moving from semi-legality to outright illegality and back again. As Sam Allende says in his marvellous business book *Be More Pirate*: 'Legal, illegal, pirate, privateer, hero, hanged, rinse, repeat'.[15] Now this variable interpretation of crime bred in Guernsey privateer crews a sort of casual attitude towards rules and regulations; during the peaceful times they were able to turn to smuggling as an alternative form of employment.

Thirdly, privateering was a form of entrepreneurship that filtered down from the merchant investors to the crews of the ships, who learned the benefits of individual action and self-fulfilment. They were becoming freelancers, piloting their own futures without the interference of the local nobility. Guernsey men and women were learning an independence of spirit that will crop up time and again in this book.

The End of Privateering

Privateers operated out of Guernsey throughout the 18th century, peaking at the key Anglo-French wars. But like all good things, the end of this slightly dubious activity came with the conclusion of the Napoleonic Wars and the peace treaties of 1815. As we will see later, a century of privateering activity had brought many new industries into the island, and trained a population in skills and attitudes that would immediately be transferred to new businesses. More of that later, but first let's turn to another allied profession that helped the island economically during the 1700s.

The Triggers that Started Smuggling

Smuggling and the creation of the St Peter Port entrepôt, were two forms of commerce brought into life by the Navigation Acts of Parliament, first enacted in the mid 17th century, and subsequently updated on a regular basis until they were repealed in 1849. Simply put, these laws aimed to protect British commercial activity by placing an external barrier around exchanges between the English colonies and the mother country. So only British ships could deliver manufactured goods to the colonies, and only British ships could bring colonial raw materials back to the UK. It was protectionism pure and simple.

This significant barrier to free trade was an opportunity for Guernsey, and not for the first or last time, the island was able to take advantage of what we could call the Guernsey loophole. The island was considered part of Great Britain, and allowed to send goods to the UK, free of any duties. But in addition, St Peter Port, as a free port, could interact with nations prohibited from dealing directly with British merchants. In today's marketing parlance, we could say that the island discovered a niche market, where they were the only real player.

Guernsey took full advantage of this fact by being the place where the French, Spanish, and Dutch could bring goods for sale, and where British colonial raw materials could be traded. It was also the place where the privateer's booty could be exchanged. Of course, being Guernseymen, the locals tended to be flexible on the rules regarding where privateers' spoils should be taken. Their boats were English-built and by law that meant they were supposed to re-export any colonial goods from St Peter Port to the mainland. Well, that second part was ignored, leaving British customs officials unsure what to do. The UK government helped them out in 1744 by stating very clearly: 'No one should bring from the Channel Islands into any port of the kingdom products from the English colonies'.[16] This certainly helped to increase smuggling. The Guernsey loophole may have created the infrastructure that was to help smooth the way for the smuggling industry, but it took another UK government decision to spark it into life.

The foreign wars of the 18th century, which were all about who controlled the seas, and who would win in the fight for colonies, were not cheap. And to pay for them, the politicians in Westminster decided that the taxpayer should foot the bill. To do so, they began placing serious taxes on many of the imported colonial products on which the British consumer had become addicted. Tea, coffee, or chocolate to drink, wines and ports to imbibe, sugar to add to hot drinks, tobacco to smoke, chew or sniff, spices to provide piquancy to bland British food, and silks to clothe the Georgian dandy.

Tea for example had a 119% import duty. Tobacco import taxes rose from 2d per pound to 5d per pound in 1685 – an increase of 150%. French brandy had a duty of £35 per ton (in today's money probably around £5,000). This would mean an excise tax on a litre of brandy of about £5 in 18th century money, and that would represent 18 weeks' salary for a labourer, or a week's wages for a middle-class professional worker.

What impact did these levels of tax have on consumption? If we just look at wine, the historian John Nye[17] has calculated that the market share of French wine out of total wine imports into the UK was 70% in the 1680s, but after punitive excise taxes, this reduced to 3% by 1720. He goes on to say that as the British couldn't afford their favourite Bordeaux wines, they switched to beer and spirits, and the taxes on them accounted for nearly 40% of the British treasury income per year. Not surprisingly, he concludes that the British paid for their government's 18th century wars in their local pubs.

The Navigation Laws provided the opportunity for Guernsey to exploit its unique loophole of lacking any constraints on exporting to the UK. At the same time, Guernsey had no limitations on trading with continental adversaries. The actual spark though, that set alight the smuggling business, was the British government's imposition of taxes on all the commodities that the average 18th century British consumer wanted to enjoy.

Smuggling, like many other acts of piracy, was a form of revolt by the ordinary people against its government and rules they felt were unfair. Whilst the Navigation Act and the crippling government taxes created the potential for smuggling, it was a widespread willingness of the working and middle-classes to disobey the 'rules' that created a profitable business for Guernsey smugglers and their English partners.

2: The Slightly Naughty Century

The Scale of the Guernsey Smuggling Industry

Smuggling became big business in the 18th century, but few records exist about its scope and finances. Not surprising, really, as it was illegal and from 1746, a capital offence. The only real mentions in historical documents are for successful captures of smugglers – and we can be pretty sure that they were just the tip of the iceberg.

There are occasional statistics that can help us understand how big smuggling was, particularly on tea. For example, a 1745 Parliamentary Committee reckoned that 3 million lbs of tea were smuggled into the UK annually – against just 1 million lbs imported legally! And between 1773–1782 this illegal importation of tea had risen to 7.5 million lbs – over 40% of the estimated 18 million lbs consumed in Britain and Ireland. Prime Minister Pitt the Younger reckoned that of the 13 million lbs of tea consumed in Britain in 1784, only 5.5 million were brought in legally! Of course, it's important to add that politicians tended to exaggerate in the pursuit of their objectives! To make it really simple, if we index the cost of imported tea, plus the tea seller's margin at 100, then the final post-tax price to the average consumer was 200. No wonder smuggling became big business. And indeed, no wonder that William Pitt slashed the tax on tea in 1784 from 119% to 12.5%. This made legal tea far more attractive and pretty much killed tea smuggling overnight.

Paul Monod in his article on smuggling during the years 1690–1760,[18] noted that smuggling was 'big business' and reckoned it accounted for one third of all trade between England and France/Holland. And Peter Girard in 1986, wrote that smuggling: 'deprived the crown of well over £1 million in 1798 – that is £15–20 million at today's money'.[19]

As late as 1807, the UK Treasury said about Guernsey and the size of its smuggling business: 'from which island alone in the course of four months of the last winter, spirits and other items were clandestinely introduced into this kingdom the duties upon which would have amounted to the sum of not less than £500,000' (Around £32 million in today's money).[20]

We can sum up the importance of smuggling on the economy of Guernsey with this quotation from the 1973 book on smuggling by David Phillipson: 'Throughout the eighteenth century and well into the nineteenth, the Channel Islands and Guernsey in particular, were an entrepôt for contraband goods. By 1750, virtually the entire economy of the island was built upon the transhipment and warehousing of goods destined for the holds of smuggling craft from the south of England'.[21]

The Logistics of Smuggling

We can look upon Guernsey as one of the hubs of the smuggling business. If French wine and brandy makers found themselves taxed out of the British market by high import duties, then St Peter Port represented a welcoming home, for not only French products but also tobacco, silk and tea. It was also where the privateers would land their booty – coming from attacks on local French vessels or larger galleons coming from the Caribbean or the East Indies. The town was a sort of warehouse for goods to be smuggled into the UK. Berry noted in 1815: 'on the return of peace, the inhabitants were induced to import and keep in store the goods which they knew to be in such demand, and which accordingly continued to attract the English smugglers'.[22]

So, the product was available. The next job was to find a customer. Here the growing merchant class of the UK (and Guernsey) played a key role as intermediaries. As Paul Monod notes 'it was not the landowners but merchants who provided the money that made smuggling into a big business'.[23] They were used to finding clients and sourcing their needs, smuggling just represented the same thing but more sneakily. They would work out what products were wanted, identify a trader in St Peter Port who had the merchandise, fund a ship and crew to bring it across the Channel (sometimes just piggy backing on a privateer's voyage), and finally, in the UK, get a team to bring it ashore and transport the goods to the customers.

In southern England, starting from around 1714, smugglers were organised in gangs – usually labourers whose low wages could be supplemented with lucrative work as part of the smuggling gang. A night's work heaving barrels of brandy from the seashore inland could earn a farm labourer more than a month's effort in the fields.

Often called 'owlers' (because like owls they operated at night), many gangs originally learned their craft illegally exporting wool from the UK to France. Later on, though, some of them established a nice round-trip business, taking wool from the south coast to the knitters of Guernsey and bringing back brandy, wine, tea and silks from the island for illegal distribution on the mainland. And these gangs could be quite large – certainly big enough to see off any customs officials.

Smuggling – The Risks

Was it a dangerous profession? What few records exist would lead one to the conclusion that smugglers were regularly trapped by the authorities. The truth though is that to police the whole of the English and Welsh coastlines – a combined length of more than 3,600 miles, as late as 1809, the Government had only 39 revenue cutters (small lightly armed boats) and 62 other vessels – so about 100 in total or one for every 36 miles of coast. This looks like pretty good odds for the smugglers – especially if you practised your business in the west country where the isolated bays were perfect for secret practices. As the collector of customs at Penzance claimed in 1804: 'The smuggling practised on this coast ... has been carried on to the greatest extent imaginable, for this last summer by luggers, sloops and other small craft from the island of Guernsey'.[24]

The Impact on Guernsey of Smuggling

Goods from France, from privateers, from the colonies, came in increasing amounts into Guernsey during the 18th century. The landed material was in bulk, and had to be broken down into manageable sizes for the smugglers, who had to manhandle the contraband ashore from ships lying off the coast in secluded bays along the English coast. This led to the creation of a number of interesting service industries in St Peter Port. One that I particularly like is what were called 'half ankers'. These were mini wooden kegs, designed and built by Guernsey coopers, to hold spirits. The mini barrels sat on the chests and backs of smugglers called 'tubmen', and were held in place by a loop of rope around the smuggler's neck. This made it far easier for men to wade ashore, climb up cliffs, and then hang the mini barrels across the backs of horses for onward transport. In addition to this barrel creation by coopers, smuggling provided good work for carpenters to create chests, labourers to carry material onto the smuggler's boats, warehouses to hold the contraband, and auctioneers to sell the produce.

2: THE SLIGHTLY NAUGHTY CENTURY

Smuggling – The End

Of course, it couldn't last. Not for the first or last time in Guernsey's economic history, the benefits of bad government policy (the restrictive mercantile high tax and protection regime) were eventually replaced with a pendulum that swung the other way.

Pitt's 1784 Commutation Act started the ball rolling by cutting tea duties down to 12.5% and essentially killed tea smuggling overnight. Next came much stricter anti-smuggling laws. The UK government calculated that halting the smugglers could bring in £1 million to the exchequer (£60 million in today's money), and so with three acts (in 1805, 1807 and 1825), the UK forced the Channel Islands into obeying the customs laws.

The final blow to smuggling came when Sir Robert Peel, as Prime Minister in the 1840s, oversaw the removal of some 1,200 tariffs on imports. At a stroke, it made Guernsey's free trade environment pretty much redundant; a victory for ordinary consumers who had rebelled against high taxes and supported the smuggling activities.

It can be argued, that smuggling from centres like Guernsey, created the consumer-driven economy that we know today. Smugglers provided enjoyable, but not essential, treats for those who could afford them. And on that subject, there is a lovely, exasperated quote from the diary of Thomas Turner, a shopkeeper in the Sussex village of East Hoathly, who wrote: 'The too frequent use of spiritous liquors and the exorbitant practice of tea drinking corrupted ... people of almost all ranks'.[25]

So the island lost a very lucrative business but, as we have already discovered, Guernsey has the incredible facility of being an economic phoenix – somehow always rising from the ashes of a trashed business model.

3: The Industry That Left No Trace

It's 1815, the Napoleonic Wars are over. Peace has spread across the world. And the people of Guernsey are not very happy. They just had a glorious century of attacking, and ransacking French and Spanish ships, with the booty coming back to the island for the sale and enrichment of the locals, who turned St Peter Port from a rather rustic, ramshackle sort of town into the elegant, opulent streets of today's island capital. Now, at the beginning of the 19th century, the semi-legal business of privateering is no longer condoned by parliament. The lucrative smuggling industry is being killed by big reductions in tax on all those little treats from abroad, plus increasingly effective customs officer interventions locally. And if all that wasn't enough, the end of the Napoleonic Wars meant the large garrison on the island was disbanded, the naval squadron disappeared, and all the French exiles were able to go home.

What was the island to do? What would become of their sailors, ships, and onshore repair yards? How would all the locals, supporting the soldiers, naval ships, and rich French refugees now make a living? How would the island avoid a massive depression? Luckily, three things helped overcome the loss of all these sources of income.

First the peace in 1815 meant trade with no hassle, no pirates, no danger. The problem for the British and French was that they were left with few boats to carry the trade to and from their empires. They had done such a good job fighting each other, that neither had much of a fleet. Guernsey however did. According to Berry, Guernsey had a fleet of 93 vessels in 1813:[1] lots of privateer boats with experienced crews. They were now ready to seek out the world's products and bring them back to Europe – which

3: The Industry That Left No Trace

they duly did, in the early years of peace, as France and Britain struggled to rebuild their fleets. As Tupper notes in 1837: 'with but little opposition from the commercial marine of the continent which had been, in great measure, destroyed during the war, and could not be immediately replaced'.[2]

A second positive for Guernsey after 1815, was the need by the UK to replace its fleet of merchant ships. Here again, the UK Government intervened in a positive way – at least for Guernsey. Laws were passed putting penalising duties on imported timber to protect the British lumber industry, the crucial supplier of raw material for boatbuilding. The Channel Islands were excluded from this legislation, which meant that Guernsey could import Scandinavian pine and French oak with no duties and thus undercut the mainland's shipbuilding industry. As noted by JM MacCulloch in 1837: 'All sorts of timber and cordage being admitted duty free into the islands, we need not wonder that great numbers of vessels are now annually built in them'.[3]

Thirdly, at the end of the Napoleonic Wars, Guernsey's quarrying industry amounted to just 6,000 tons of granite exported to the UK. By 1835 this had grown 800% to 54,000 tons and by 1854, a further 120% to 120,000 tons. The stone from Guernsey quarries needed to be carried to the UK – mainly London – and that meant ships. Enough of them to carry just under 2,500 tons of granite a week.

So, despite the fact that Guernsey had rarely built any ships prior to 1815 (apart from fishing boats), the scene was set for nearly a century of serious boat-building activity along the east coast of the island. Activity driven by Guernsey merchants, keen to exploit the exciting prospect of opening up trade routes with the Americas, the Far East and the Azores, plus the seemingly never-ending demand from London, for more and more granite for their roads and pavements.

As Berry says, in his *History of Guernsey* in 1815, about the local shipbuilding activities: 'If the number of ships and merchants were to increase tenfold, they would, in the present state of the world, find ample employment'.[4] And guess what? The island in 1804 already had 103 shipwrights, working in the yards of four repair companies (Liverpool, a much bigger town, at the same time had 487). Many of these shipwrights were English, and after 1815, set about teaching the locals how to build ships.

The island also had rope makers and sail repairers. It had blacksmiths. And especially, it had the wood-handling skills of coopers who had made transportable containers of wines and tobacco during the 18th century. And now, thanks to the British government and its protective policies, the island could import low-cost French oak and Scandinavian pine, unlike its British competitors. Lastly, it had cheap labour compared to the mainland (a shipwright was 3/6d a day in Guernsey but 4/– in Sunderland: 12.5% less). In fairness it's also relevant to point out that labour was even cheaper in Jersey and indeed they built significantly more ships.

Finally, the local merchants also realised that building big wooden ships required no serious capital investment. Ships in those days were essentially built by hand and just needed space and a slip down to the sea for launches. As Eric Sharp noted in 1970: 'Ships were built on open beaches, on fields bordering streams — anywhere within reach of tide water'.[5]

'Let's get on with it!' came the cry from local businessmen, and in the four years (1815–1819) following the end of the Napoleonic Wars, the island built and launched 20 ocean-going ships. These were mainly for trade with Latin America, with 30 more coming off the launching slips in the subsequent four years 'because it was cheaper than buying elsewhere'.[6] In the 14 years from 1812 to 1828, the island's shipbuilders constructed 68 vessels: 4 ships,

3: The Industry That Left No Trace

26 brigs, 3 schooners, plus 35 sloops and cutters.[7] And on it went for the next 50 or so years, with 300 ships of up to 656 tons being constructed or lengthened between 1815 and 1878. Little, 24 square mile Guernsey became one of the important shipbuilding centres for the whole of the British Isles.

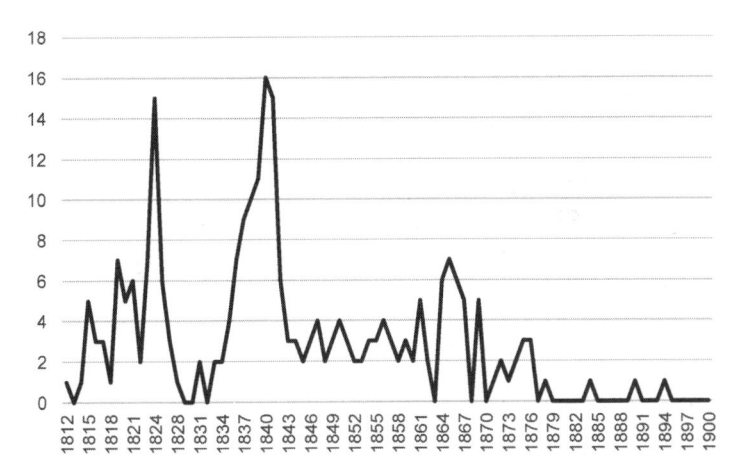

Fig 2: Ships built, 1812–1900.
(See Appendix for sources)

There are many references in the history books to these different types of boat built in Guernsey – but what exactly do they mean?

The biggest were ships, which had three or more masts, and were what they called 'fully-rigged' (lots of sails). Next came barques; they also had three or more masts and were called the 'workhorse' of 19th century cargo transportation. They had square sails and could work with smaller crews than ships. A bit further down in size were schooners, with two or three same height masts, and were about 100 tons in size. They may have been small, but they were fast – helpful if you were bringing perishable oranges from the south. Then, there were the brigs with two masts and square sails. They had been popular with pirates and privateers because of their speed and manoeuvrability. Still smaller were cutters, with mostly just one mast: small and speedy and popular with smugglers. They were around 24 metres long and weighed up to 150 tons. Equally popular with pirates and smugglers were the smallest sailing boats, the sloop, with a single mast and measuring up to 18 metres in length.

When Were the Ships Built?

There seem to have been three peak periods for shipbuilding on the island, each lasting about ten years. The first was immediately after the Napoleonic Wars, from 1815 to 1825, when 60 ships were launched along the east coast. The second burst happened between 1835 and 1845, when an incredible 86 vessels came out of Guernsey yards. And a final hooray happened in the decade from 1860 to 1870, when 38 ships were launched. Indeed, it appears that 1864 was the peak year for Channel Islands shipbuilding, with the two islands 'contributing 6% to the total tonnage of wooden sailing vessels built in the UK'.[8] We can take a guess at what stimulated these three phases of shipbuilding. The first phase was triggered by the general absence of enough vessels to meet the explosion of free trade after 1815, both across the European continent, as well as further afield in South America. According to Tupper writing in 1837, 19 schooners were built in the 1820s, for the London fruit trade (from the Mediterranean). Sharp, in his article on shipbuilding, also references the need for boats to handle a local booming oyster-dredging business.[9]

The second period may well have been stimulated by a drop off in the Latin American trade 'due to competition from France, Genoa and Sardinia'[10] and the need for fast schooners for the fresh fruit trade with Spain and Portugal. The third phase coincides with a serious jump in granite exports (1852–1875), resulting in an increase of just under 200% in shipments. This last phase also happened in a period when trade with Australia, India, the Far East and Costa Rica (for coffee) was being opened up. Finally, according to Victor Coysh, the last sailing vessel built in Guernsey was the ketch *Sarnia* in 1894.[11]

Where Were the Shipyards?

Walking along the east coast from the Val des Terres to St Sampson's, a distance of just three miles (5 km), you'd think there would be some vestige of an industry that launched nearly 300 ships (291) in just 60 years. After all, the island is littered with derelict greenhouses. It's hard not to come across huge holes today from the granite export industry. We can even find plenty of structures from our Neolithic forebears going back more than 5,000 years.

But shipbuilding? Almost nothing is left, apart from a few murky photographs held in the Priaulx Library which show sites up and down the east coast, not surprising, as this is where Guernsey men had spent much of the 18th century, patching up, repairing and refitting ships for smugglers and privateers. Even peering closely at the first Ordnance Survey map of 1898, it's difficult to find traces of shipbuilding.

But it was indeed the east coast where the shipbuilding took place. Off this coast was deep water, it had steeply sloping shingle beaches (in St Peter Port), two harbours for the reception of raw materials, sort of half-decent roads for carting in the wood, rope, metal, and tar, plus plenty of labour at hand from the smuggling/privateering/entrepôt industries.

In 1970, Eric Sharp wrote a wonderful history of the Guernsey shipbuilding industry for La Société Guernesiaise. In it, he identified the main areas for shipbuilding. The first was from the bottom of the Val des Terres along to just before the Town Church – a short distance that you can drive today in less than 30 seconds. Despite its minuscule area, the four yards here constructed an amazing 70 ships. And already on a map of the town in 1843, John Wood, the surveyor, printed on his plan 'ships, docks and building yards' by Havelet Bay. The second area, also in St Peter Port, was at the North Beach. Back in the early 19th century, there was a steeply sloping beach here – good for launching the 19 ships constructed here. Productive it might have been, but shipbuilding stopped here in 1854 due to the completion of the North Esplanade, which cut off the shipyards from the sea.

Area three was from the bottom of St Julian's Avenue up to the start of Belle Greve Bay. Here there were seven yards, contributing some of the largest and fastest ships built on the island. This area included Guernsey's oldest shipbuilding yard: Barry Le Patourel, which was founded in 1815.

In 1926, the *Guernsey Free Churchman* magazine interviewed an 80-year-old, who recounted his memories of this shipbuilding area:

> It is interesting to note that in those days, on account of the level nature of the shipyard, the only method of launching was by means of wooden rollers, the ship being held back by huge blocks attached by strong tackle.[12]

The fourth area was St Sampson's, which had seven yards, all clustered around the harbour, including the most famous shipbuilder of the island – Peter Ogier, who constructed Guernsey's largest ship, the *Golden Spur*, weighing in at 656 tons with a length of 200 feet. It competed with the famous *Cutty Sark* for the China tea business.

3: The Industry That Left No Trace

What Did the Shipyards Look Like?

They were fairly rudimentary. A shed to hold materials. A slipway to launch the hand-built vessels. Maybe timber poles to facilitate launching if the yard was on flat land. Long staves to hold the ship during construction. Sometimes the ship under construction would have a canopy over it to ensure work could carry on whatever the weather. The photographs that still exist show these yards were messy-looking places.

Who Were the Shipbuilders?

These shipyards built boats for Guernsey entrepreneurs although some did get orders from the UK. The owners of the shipyards seemed to have been a mix of local craftsmen and English immigrants.

Thanks to local historian Eric Sharp, we know the names of the various companies engaged in shipbuilding. The St Peter Port builders included: De la Mare; de Putron and Vaudin; Perret; W. Jones, all by Havelet Bay. Machon at North Beach; Barry Le Patourel by St Julians Avenue; Sullock, King and Thomson on Glategny; Alexander Thom at La Piette; Rankilor and Brouard by the Longstore and James Sebire near Hougue à la Père.

Then at St Sampson's were: Stonelakes; Rankilor (with their second yard on the east coast); Thom (also here with a second yard); Ledstone; Peter Ogier; Domaille and Brache; and Sauvarin.

Were These Shipbuilders Any Good?

An average of four ships were built each year from the end of the Napoleonic Wars and the 1870s. The shipbuilders had low-cost timber, cheapish labour and handy sites for launches. So, did they take advantage of their low production costs and go for a low-price approach? It seems not, as Guernsey-built ships received praise from all over the world for their high quality. So, yet another Guernsey 'brand' had been created.

A Spanish newspaper in 1870 declared: 'The ship brokers of Santander say the *Island Belle* has been for the past week, the talk and admiration of the port. Mr Peter Ogier of St Sampson's was the builder'.[13] And a local paper recorded the following description of the fruiter *Jessie* in 1840: 'in strength of construction, like most Guernsey vessels, she is far superior to most vessels built elsewhere'.[14]

Perhaps more practical is the fact that according to Tupper in 1837: 'Channel Island built vessels have acquired so good a name at Lloyds that insurances by them are frequently effected on better terms than other equally well founded British or foreign vessels'.[15] And lastly, none other than Victor Hugo (a Guernsey resident for many years) declared: 'The maritime carpentry of Guernsey is renowned'.[16]

Even though Guernsey boats were solid and well-constructed, reviewing what happened to the 291 ships built in the 19th century, it's clear that sailing in those days was a precarious occupation. It looks like 132 of these vessels were wrecked, sunk or missing.[17]

Who Owned or Commissioned the Boats?

Just because Guernsey had the skills, low-cost production and good access to safe deep water, this did not mean it was inevitable that it would become a shipbuilding island. It needed clients who wanted the ships that they could build. And it seemed most of the demand came from local merchants. According to Jamieson and his diligent research, 1,238 people owned shares in Guernsey boats between 1817–1890, and three quarters of them lived on the island.

3: The Industry That Left No Trace

It's not surprising that the local merchants pushed for locally-built craft. Guernsey is an island and before the aeroplane, everything that was needed to support the local population had to come by sea – excluding local farm produce. So, it wasn't just a good idea to build ships to access world trade. It was vital just to ensure the Guernsey people could eat, work and play.

What Did the Ships Carry?

Initially, the Guernsey merchants and their ships concentrated on taking wine and spirits from Spain and Portugal to South America, returning to European ports with coffee, sugar and animal hides amongst other things. Unfortunately, from the 1840s, this business declined due to increased competition, and so local ship owners switched either to the fruit trade from the Azores and the Iberian Peninsula (in 1845 just over 50% of foreign trade came from these two regions), or to shipping stone from the quarries in the north of the island, in large sturdy ships to the mainland.

We can get a snapshot of the variety of cargoes arriving in island as noted by *The Star* newspaper in 1828:

December 24: *Minerva*, Jones, Weymouth, ballast. *Two Brothers*, Salsbury, Brixham, ballast. *Diana*, Stone, Jersey, fruit, &c. 25: *Mercury*, Pearce, Bremen, timber. *Aeolus*, Priaulx, Southampton, hops. &c. 26: Steam-packet *Ivanhoe*, White, Jersey, ballast. *Frederick*, Kellaway, Alderney, ballast. *Peggy*, Perchard, Jersey, bark, &c. 27: Steam-packet *Watersprite*, White, Weymouth, ballast. *St Pierre*, Cleret, Havre, vitriol. 28: *Brilliant*, Brouard, London, sundries. *Mars*, Fortin, Cherbourg, cattle. *Actif*, Darthenay, St Malo, cattle. *Mary*, Amlod, Poole, stones. *Friendship*, Shean, Lyme, sailcloth. *Beverley*, Eiley, Newcastle, coals. *Liberty*, Watson, Newcastle, coals. *Good*

Intent, Domaille, Newcastle, coals. *General Doyle*, Le Couvet, Jersey, wines. *Julia*, White, Portsmouth, ballast. 29: Steam-packet *Watersprite*, White, Jersey, ballast. *Adventure*, Luce, London, sundries. *Diligent*, Porter, Southampton, bale-goods. *Experiment*, Deslandes, Alderney, ballast. *Samuel & Julia*, Garland, Weymouth, sailcloth. 30: Steam-packet *Ivanhoe*, Conner, Weymouth, ballast. *Proteus*, Nissen, Copenhagen, wheat and barley. *Juliana*, Richardson, Newcastle, coals. *L'Hirondelle*, Tirel, Cherbourg, ballast. *Diligent*, Pilant, Cherbourg, ballast.[18]

Why Did Shipbuilding Die?

In the short term, a depression in world trade from the late 1860s put a big brake on the continued expansion of shipbuilding, with freight rates dropping, leading to reduced profits for ship owners. But the real killer was technology. Since the 1820s, iron had begun to replace wood as the shipbuilding material of choice, and once combined with steam rather than wind, well – the story begins to have an inevitable conclusion. Steam-powered ships could operate whatever the weather. Iron hulls were sturdier, cheaper to produce and could carry larger loads.

But for Guernsey shipbuilders, this new technology was too difficult to embrace for an island far from iron-producing areas, and too small to cope with the big sites needed for building iron-clad ships. The very artisanal nature of Guernsey's shipbuilding century, means that today there is almost no evidence of its existence.

But were the islanders scratching their heads about what to do next to earn their living? Apparently not, as those heads were being turned by the booming quarrying business, plus both the

3: The Industry That Left No Trace

beginnings of the horticultural revolution that was to sweep across the island, and the tentative baby steps into the tourist industry.

And so, yet again, Guernsey demonstrated a willingness to drop a dying industry and explore new horizons. Resilience seems to run through the veins of the islanders. The shipbuilding century had been the midwife for a huge boom in the island's population, mostly from immigrants, attracted by work opportunities and a lower cost of living. In just 70 years (1821–1891), the island's population exploded by 75% – people who would help provide the manpower for the three industries we'll talk about next.

4: Guernsey Rocks

To start this chapter, I'd like you, the reader, to do a little bit of observation – particularly if you live in the south of England. Here is your challenge: next time you are in your local big town or maybe in London, spend some time looking down rather than up.

Look at the kerbstones that separate the pavement from the road. Are they a sort of blueish colour? If they are, then there's a good chance the stone was quarried and shaped in Guernsey. And despite their smooth surface, the kerbstones you spotted are probably between 100 and 150 years old. Oh, and underneath the tarmac surface of the road alongside the kerbstones, there is a good chance that it still has a base of Guernsey 'setts' or cobbles.

In just 100 years (1839 to 1939), Guernsey extracted and exported 4 million tons of rock from its 24 square miles, leaving

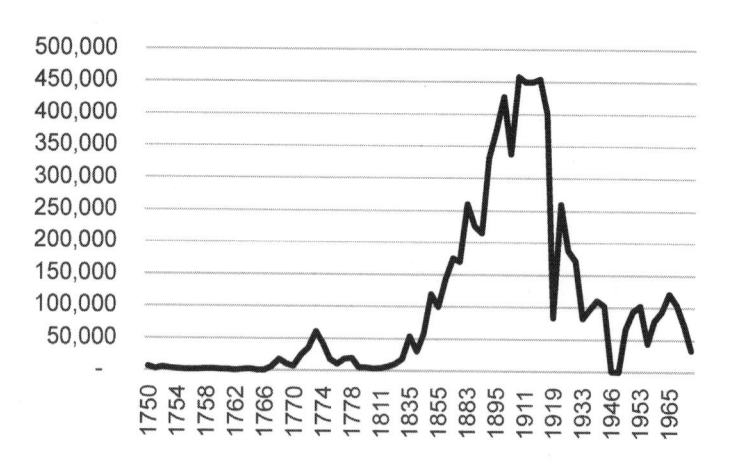

Fig 3: Stone Exports (tons), 1810–1972.
(See Appendix for sources)

a landscape that has been described as a giant colander. Walk around London today, and you will find this little island's granite footprints all over the city. From the steps of St Paul's, to the road surface of Blackfriars Bridge. From the ballast under its railway lines, to the kerbstones of its streets; the island's stone forms the virtual bedrock of one of the world's greatest cities.

Quarrying and the export of rock was Guernsey's dominant industry in the 19th century: but today, apart from one solitary site, this business has almost disappeared, leaving deep holes, filled with rainwater or rubbish bags as its very useful memorial.

Origins

So where, how, and why did this commercialisation of the island's bedrock begin? Some would say that Guernsey's Neolithic ancestors started it by excavating, shaping and positioning great lumps of stone on to their burial tombs. Others would look to the Elizabethan times, when fashion dictated that the 1,000 or more houses on the island should be faced with granite. And then there is a case for identifying the feudal obligation of every road-bordering household to maintain route surfaces. Finally, many would point the finger at a Dorset man – John Mowlem – as the original champion of the industry. His company impacted the island's look, its prosperity and even the very make-up of the population. Whatever its origins, the quarrying episode in the island's history has impacted Guernsey in physical, economic and social ways. It's a story that can be told in six episodes.

What is Guernsey Granite?

First though, what is this rock that had such a value to builders in the Victorian era? Most locals refer to it as Guernsey granite but, if we want to be picky, that's not true. Granite is made up of three key elements: quartz, feldspar and mica. And to be called 'granite', the rock must have at least 20% of its content as quartz and 35% feldspar (the word granite comes from the Latin *granum* – a grain). The island quarried two types of rock, neither of which meet the quartz or feldspar criteria. First to the north of St Sampson's there is Bordeaux Diorite and to the south of this town, down as far as St Peter Port, is St Peter Port Gabbro.[1]

Diorite is pretty rare. It is created by the slow cooling of the earth's liquid magma centre. In this process, different minerals are created and, in the case of Guernsey Diorite, this means feldspar (usually black or darkish in colour), mica and something called hornblende, which is a rock-forming series of minerals.

The coarse-grained St Peter Port Gabbro is similar in origin to diorite, but is globally a lot more common, as it makes up most of the Earth's oceanic crust. It also has the hornblende crystals in it, along with feldspar, but is poorer in its sodium atoms than diorite. It is very strong and dense, and as a result makes for a perfect material to build roads, unlike the Bordeaux Diorite which is easier to shape and is therefore good for building structures. Without getting too nerdy about it, these two rock types are special. As John Renouf put it in the *Geology Today* periodical in 1985: 'Northern Guernsey is a mecca for the igneous petrologist'.[2]

So how did these two rocks come to be found on Guernsey? The island is part of what they call the Armorican Massif, which is a geological feature of mainly north-western France. This was formed when the Bay of Biscay came into being, through a pushing and pulling of the earth's crust during the creation of the Atlantic, with Guernsey being part of the edge of a great lump of land or rift, which dropped and made this large inlet of the Atlantic Ocean.

So, having set the scene, let's now plunge into the story of the Victorian stone industry. For ease of understanding, I'll use the word 'granite' in the commercial sense, but you now know it should be the more lumbering Bordeaux Diorite and St Peter Port Gabbro.

Episode One: A Local Industry (3,000 BC – 1830)

It was a daft thing to do. I know. But when I read there were 94 quarries on the island in 1847, and 268 in 1930,[3] I wanted to know how the writers knew. So, at the Island Archives in St Peter Port I asked the team there to dig out a copy of the first OS map of the island from 1898. Then I set to counting each quarry recorded on the map – both those just indicated as 'quarry' and those marked 'quarry – disused'.

I did it carefully, missing perhaps the odd one or two, but I can say authoritatively that there were 329 quarries on the 1898 map. And my guess is the figure of 94 in 1847, was pretty much that number back in 1830, at the end of this first period. So, between Neolithic man and the beginnings of Victoria's reign, why and how were there already nearly one hundred quarries on the island?

You can see prehistoric man's quarrying efforts all over Guernsey, or more precisely, their graves. Great lumps of rock, roughly hammered into shape, sitting on top of boulder-lined burial chambers. And like many relics of prehistory, these monuments raise the question – how on earth did they do it? 'Quarrying' is probably a misnomer for how Neolithic man acquired their burial capping stones. Probably 'found and moved' is a better way to describe their activities.

Things got a bit more professional in Roman Guernsey, or Lisia as it may have been known to them. It's only relatively recently that we are beginning to discover bits and pieces of the

Roman occupation of the island. We know they anchored off St Peter Port, thanks to the discovery of the Roman vessel, nicknamed *Asterix*, back in the 1980s. St Peter Port was the only decent natural harbour, or rather roadstead (an area of sea safe to anchor as it was protected from swells, rip tides and other tricky sea conditions) in the Channel Islands; and the Romans, who liked to sail within sight of land, clearly appreciated its safety – plus the added benefits of fresh water and salt from La Salerie for preserving food on route.

It's well documented that Romans were great quarrymen – indeed the word 'quarry' has a Latin origin. And at the famous Roman villa in Fishbourne, West Sussex, archaeologists have found Guernsey Granite. So clearly the island's stone was already appearing outside Guernsey over 2,000 years ago.

After the Romans withdrew from the islands, it's likely that very little quarrying took place in Guernsey until it became part of mainland Europe's continental church. This led to the building of many stone churches in the 11th–13th centuries – replacing older wooden structures.

In fact, wood was in short supply in Guernsey for the inhabitants, and so it's likely that houses and commercial structures were all built with shaped granite from little quarries dotted around the island. And the skill to dress this granite is likely to have been acquired around the 15th century by copying the activities of the labourers working in the quarries near St Malo in Brittany.

By the 17th century there were 1,039 granite-built houses on the island,[4] and each was probably constructed using stone from little quarries opened just for this purpose, according to historians Fenn and Yeoman. And we do know for example that there was already a quarry at St Germain in Castel in 1639.

These quarries were given a boost by architectural fashion in the 18th century, as house owners started to reface their old buildings with posh, dressed granite blocks. The expansion of the harbour in St Peter Port gave an extra push to the quarrying business. Plus military demands for protection from the French led to the building of the loophole towers around the island's coast.

By the way, it has been suggested that the Guernsey stone export business was helped by the building of St Paul's Cathedral in the 17th century, specifically the famous west entrance steps. Well, they are indeed made from Guernsey stone (either Bordeaux Diorite or possibly granite from a little outcrop off the coast, near Jethou, called Crevichon). And they have weathered remarkably well – unlike the original steps which came from the Isle of Man, and were made from black limestone which had to be replaced, due to unexpectedly fast weathering, in the 1800s, with granite from Guernsey.

So up to the end of this quarrying episode, most stone was dug out for local consumption – for churches, homes, the harbour and military defences. But there was one final local need for stone. The Guernsey *corvée* (feudal law) required 'people with land adjacent to a roadway to keep it well maintained'.[5] This was often done using *talvaine*, which was a kind of decomposing granite consisting of small pieces of stone easily used to surface roads. As not everyone in Guernsey had easy access to stone, each parish was obliged to have at least one parochial quarry, which was used to provide households with the material needed to satisfy the *corvée*.

In addition to this local use of quarrying, the 18th century saw the rebirth of the export of stone, probably for the first time since the Romans. London as usual seems to have kick-started this. In an article on 18th century London paving, Jeffery notes that the local authorities decided in 1767, to take steps to do something about the poor quality of the thoroughfares.[6] The key part of this drive was their description of what needed to be done: 'pebble paving, which is done with stones collected from the sea beach, mostly brought from the islands of Guernsey and Jersey; they are very durable, indeed the most so of any stone used for this purpose'.[7]

Local historian Richard Hocart[8] was able to find pretty much a whole century's worth of stone export information in the National Archives, revealing that already in 1696/7, Guernsey was exporting some stone (202 tons in that year). This grew steadily throughout the 1700s, with the 1770s showing significant export figures of between 10 and 60,000 tons a year, mainly to London. And these figures include not just beach pebbles but, for the first time, separate figures for quarried paving stones.

And what London does, provincial towns often follow. In this case, Portsmouth took the lead, and we can read in their commissioner's contract the following stipulation: 'the horseways and carriageways of the said streets [shall be paved with] good new Guernsey pebbles with not less than one ton of such pebbles to four square yards'.[9]

Portsmouth's lead was in turn followed by Winchester and Southampton – and in an article by Robert Thomson we can read the local contracts which included the words 'Captain Priaux do bring from Guernsey 5 tons of Horse flatners'.[10] According to Tupper's 1876 *History of Guernsey* these were 'large pebbles only for paving, shipped from Grand Havre and Perelle Bay'.[11]

Every local historian uses this reference from Tupper, but I wanted to know why an authority in Southampton chose to get these 'pebbles' from Guernsey? After all, the south coast of England is littered with pebbly beaches – usually flint (a form of quartz), which is quite durable, and you would think would make a decent road surface.

A couple of reasons seem to make sense. First, the lousy roads of the time meant transporting 1,000 tons of rock on land would be a serious and expensive challenge. Secondly, the regular sailing-boat crossings from the island to Southampton, made Guernsey a familiar place for merchants of this Hampshire town. And thirdly, the sailing ships all carried ballast, so the idea of carrying pebbles would not have been an alien concept.

Perhaps the most important trigger for the Victorian quarrying industry came at the end of the Napoleonic Wars in 1815. Towns around the UK began to sort out the appalling state of their roads. For Guernsey granite exports, this was helped by the repeal in 1819 of duty charged on stone imported to the UK from the island.

The benefits of using dressed, rectangular setts (or cobbles) for road surfaces quickly gained traction in the UK. And in 1828–29 over 20,000 tons of granite were shipped to the UK, according to Samuel Lewis' *Topographical Dictionary* of 1833: noting that 'the island quarries afforded employment to a great number of inhabitants'.[12] Indeed the 1831 census identified 112 stone cutters and quarrymen in the Vale and St Sampson's.

These dressed stones were probably the less important of granite exports. The big demand was for pieces of granite for road surfaces, as part of the 'macadamising' system, developed by John McAdam. *The Star* newspaper, for example, reported that in 1827, 1,200 tons of paving stones were exported from the island, but over 9,400 tons of granite for road surfaces. And indeed, two years later stone chippings amounted to 25,000 tons exported to the UK.

Episode Two: The Beginnings of an Industry 1830-1850

We ended the first episode of Guernsey's dominant 19th century industry with a reference to John Louden McAdam. He should probably be considered, if not the father of the local industry, then certainly its godfather. In 1821, he wrote a key book *Remarks On The Present System Of Road Making*[13] and later presented his findings to a Parliamentary committee.

Why was Parliament so interested in roads? Well at the start of the 19th century, roads across the country were generally awful and made travelling a real nightmare. And this was particularly true of London, which was experiencing a huge growth in population: from 1714 to 1840, its population grew from 630,000 to nearly two million. It was chaos in the city. No rights of way, no observed direction rules, dust, dung, mud, ruts, fallen horses. No wonder MPs wanted answers and McAdam provided them.

He was wonderfully blunt in his observations to Parliament, and backed them up with a plethora of real examples of good and bad roads across the country. He was unimpressed with what he found and destroyed many of the road-making paradigms of the time. He was damning in his analysis of London roads. He noted that they used London gravels which contained a lot of mud, and tended to have rounded pebbles which did not lock together to make a good surface.

Instead, he proposed a completely new way of building roads (possibly adapted from the Roman method), involving the creation of three layers of stone – each constructed with decreasing sized stone. And he emphasised the need for roads to have cambers to help the quick draining of rain away from the road surface.

The size requirement was the central part of McAdam's method. The bottom layer should use stones no larger than 75mm, and the top layer with pieces no bigger than 20mm. He went further, and instructed quarry owners to create the stones he needed by employing labourers, who were to sit with small hammers, and break the rock into units of less than 170 grams. Apparently, the practical way that Guernsey stone workers judged if they had got the right size, was to try to put them in their mouths!

His submission to Parliament in March 1819[14] contained the most telling and far-reaching statements for Guernsey's future industry: 'Granite chippings might be obtained occasionally from

Cornwall, Guernsey and Scotland, as ballast'. And: 'London is placed in a situation peculiarly convenient for being supplied with materials from a distance, by water carriage'. So, Guernsey granite was specifically mentioned, and delivery by water recommended.

Guernsey had an advantage over the other two sources of granite, mentioned by McAdam. It was nearer to London. Aberdeen is 483 nautical miles away from the port of London, and Falmouth in Cornwall, 372 nautical miles. In comparison, the stone exporting port of St Sampson's is only 357 nautical miles. That meant Guernsey granite could be in the capital nearly a day sooner, and pay fewer shipping charges. Plus, the use of land transport was far more expensive than by sea (remember the terrible state of the roads at the time).

To give you an idea of the importance of this shipping benefit, in 1837, 320 sailing ships loaded at St Sampson's, with 30,000 tons of stone – an average of 93 tons per ship.[15] And by 1852, this had risen to 542 ships loading just under 59,000 tons of stone. That's something like 12 ships a day, each mooring and loading in, say, an hour of daylight. No wonder this second town of the island was growing so quickly.

Another factor, McAdam considered, was the toughness of Guernsey granite. In 1829–30, a little later than his parliamentary exposition, an experiment took place along the Commercial Road in London. This route went from the growing docks area in the East End, towards the City of London. The test was conducted to help cope with the enormous amount of traffic passing along the road from the docks. Essentially, they built a stone 'tramway' using Guernsey, Aberdeen and Cornish granite slabs, 46 centimetres wide, 30 centimetres deep and up to 3 metres long, on which massive vehicles could be more easily hauled by a horse.

The slabs of granite were weighed before being positioned and then, 17 months later, taken up and weighed again. In less than one and a half years, the Aberdeen granite had lost over 6 kilos, the Cornish granite over 5 kilos but the Guernsey granite only 2 kilos. In other words, the island's stone was three times tougher.[16]

Aberdeen granite was Guernsey's nemesis and remained so throughout the 19th century, despite these statistics. No doubt the Guernsey stone merchants made the most of this weakness, compounded by another piece of market research done at the time. Again in the Commercial Road, where it was shown that in four years, the Aberdeen granite lost 10 centimetres in height through wear and tear.

So, there were some significant commercial benefits for getting London's thoroughfares paved with Guernsey granite – if you were astute enough to be aware of them. And that brings us to one of the true fathers of the island's quarrying business – John Mowlem.

Mowlem was born in Swanage, Dorset, the son of a quarryman, and spent his teenage years working in the quarries on the Isle of Purbeck.[17] Quite remarkably for the times, this teenager, at the age of 19, took the enormously brave step of moving to London, where he worked for Henry Westmacott, the Government mason and builder. He eventually became his foreman 'over all the works then going on in London'.[18]

Driven by the irritating management style of Westmacott ('he was a shabby master')[19] and seeing the huge demand for macadamising the streets of London, in 1823, Mowlem set up his own company as a paving contractor and stone merchant, creating his own unloading wharf where the Victoria Station forecourt is now situated. Here he brought ashore limestone from Purbeck, sandstone from York, and granite from both Aberdeen and Guernsey. Throughout the 1830s, he completed paving contracts in London, and despite intense competition and low margins, managed to build a profitable business. It is interesting that when he started his company, John McAdam was one of his backers.

No doubt his good reputation helped him win his first major contract in 1839 – the re-surfacing of Blackfriars Bridge, which used Guernsey granite setts or 'narrow cubes' as they were known, measuring 2.5cm x 15cm x 23cm in depth. They were laid on a 2.5cm bed of concrete and jointed with mortar. The size of these cubes was important, as the width was pretty much that of a horse's hoof and enabled those animals to get a grip on the surface.

In his early years in business, Mowlem had learned a hard lesson: if you don't safeguard your source of stone, you'll lose the contract. That's why in 1830, he came to Guernsey, and after trying unsuccessfully to buy granite from the key local quarry owners, he bought his own site. As he notes in his diary: 'I immediately fixed on a field, all good blue granite, about one English acre, in the north-east part of the island'.[20]

This might be a good moment to talk about how, in those early days, entrepreneurs chose their land for quarrying. They looked for *hougues* – as they were called in Guernsey French – hills or hillocks, where they could dig into the hillside, working away the earth and decomposed rock 'overburden' until the granite appeared. The historian WT Gallienne has a wonderful way of describing these *hougues*, saying they were 'like peaches with a large stone in the middle'.[21]

Back to John Mowlem and Blackfriars Bridge. This was very much a make-or-break job for his young company. In 1839, he went to the island and lived there for nine months, to supervise the quarrying and shaping of the granite setts for the bridge. As he put it in his diary: 'this contract is one of the best I have ever had and will place me above harm'.[22]

In those months, he innovated in many ways to ensure continuous production – like putting canvas over the site to ensure rain didn't stop the workers' efforts. He also raised piece rates for quarrymen and, lacking sufficient labourers, imported workers from the UK (many from Cornwall), and undercut rivals by reducing the cost of dressed stone from 4d to 3d. His 'narrow cubes' developed for Blackfriars Bridge were a new product on the market. They gave him first-mover advantages over his competitors, and helped make him one of the go-to suppliers for London parishes.

Blackfriars Bridge and Guernsey granite really put the Mowlem company on the map. Contracts came pouring in: paving St Clement Danes, maintaining government properties in the capital, repaving London Bridge and the Strand, and providing some of the granite setts for the Thames Embankment. Indeed by 1848, most streets in the City of London were cobbled with granite setts.

Despite retiring in 1845, John Mowlem continued to watch over his Guernsey quarries – buying two further sites in 1848. This probably reflected the huge demand for granite he had had to cope with in the previous year – 50,000 tons had been needed. And reflecting yet again, his belief in the vertical integration of his business, Mowlem had sailing ships called *John Mowlem* built in St Sampson's – the first in 1841.

These sailing ships, loaded with granite, needed a decent place to unload, and Mowlem's company signed a lease in 1852 for a site called Millbank, on the south side of the Thames in Greenwich. This eventually became known as Granite Wharf and was owned by the company into the 21st century. The rock unloaded here was then put into barges, and taken further up the Thames to Mowlem's wharves in Pimlico, Westminster and Blackfriars. Some of the roads near Granite Wharf are now legally protected because of their original Guernsey Blue Diorite cobbled surfaces.

So, by the end of this second chapter in the history of Guernsey's quarrying industry, the pioneer John Mowlem had elevated Guernsey granite to the material of choice – or 'brand'

– for many highway improvement projects in the capital. He had innovated production processes and created a fully vertically integrated business, from quarry to shipping to construction.

His choice of projects set the seal on the way Guernsey granite was used over the next 100 years. Mowlem chose a niche in the market – the use of Guernsey granite chippings as the base for macadamising roads. It was an unglamorous choice but extremely effective, and was eventually extended to the foundations for railway tracks as well. Mowlem had a contract with railways in south-east England for 6.5 centimetre ballast 'for many years'.[23]

His success did not go unnoticed. The poor economic conditions for agricultural workers on the mainland provided the impetus for others to seek their fortunes in the Guernsey granite business. Future leaders of the industry arrived by 1851 – Messrs Hamley, Stranger and Fry. And not only entrepreneurs – the population of the island almost doubled between 1800 and 1851, from 16,155 to 30,000. Many had come to work in the quarries or the stone-breaking mills. Nevertheless, despite this boom, at the end of 1851, quarrying still only accounted for 6.3% of the working population – but in our next section, we'll see this was to change significantly.

Episode Three: The Early Boom Years 1850–1880

Throughout Guernsey's commercial history, local or national government legislation has played an important role, in either helping or hindering growth. In 1847, the still-youthful granite export business got a shot in the arm with the repeal of the law that stone for macadamising had to be broken within 32 kilometres of London. That year saw the island working 94 quarries.

Another positive political event helped the industry at the halfway mark of the 19th century. The Great Exhibition at the

Crystal Palace was a wonderful shop window for all things British – and Guernsey made sure it was present.

The official invitation to Guernsey inhabitants to participate in Prince Albert's brainchild was printed in *The Star* newspaper, on Saturday 30 March 1850. A committee was formed, and worked out what local products should be featured for display at this remarkable showcase.

Amongst the items sent from Guernsey were the following rock specimens:

- Porphyritic Gneiss, from Pleinmont Cliffs.
- Red Porphyritic Gneiss, from the same.
- Black Hornblende, from the same.
- Hornblende Schist, from Castel au Roc.
- Red Syenite, from Roc de Guet.
- Grey Syenite, from Mont Cuet.
- Blue Syenite, from the Vale quarries.
- Grey Syenite, from the island of Herm.
- Porphyry (black), from the island of Sark.
- Steatite, from the same island.

These rock samples were apparently supplied by Thomas Glugas junior, and joined 62 other mining and mineral displays shown at the Crystal Palace.[24]

At the start of the second half of the 19th century, the industry was taking great chunks out of the island, and importing large numbers of labourers from the southwest of England, from potato-blight stricken Ireland and from the west of France. What's surprising is that very few islanders really knew the extent of this industry. In 1869, *The Star* wrote: 'While the stone trade has been so material an element in our commerce, its existence has scarcely been known to generations of our population'. And reading the beautiful copperplate writing of the minute taker of the Guernsey

Chamber of Commerce, throughout the middle years of Victoria's reign, there is almost no mention, apart from annual export statistics, of an industry that, in 1861, was employing ten percent of the working population.

There is a reason for this reticence. The quarrying and stone export business was not entirely in the hands of Guernseymen. John Mowlem and the entrepreneurs who followed him, were from the UK. Yes, they paid local labourers to bash up the granite lumps blown out of the ground, but profits went back to the mainland.

To understand this, we need to bring in another local industry, shipbuilding. Remember John Mowlem, building his first ship in St Sampson's? A sailing ship. And that was how granite got to London in the first half of the 19th century. Not only did the granite export business support the Guernsey shipbuilding and ship-owning businesses, but it also gave employment to the sailors on board those vessels, and to the land-side businesses of provisioning, repairing, insuring and general fitting-out of those ships.

We talked in a previous chapter about the Guernsey shipbuilding boom in the 19th century, but it pretty much came to an end by the 1880s, as steam-driven iron and steel vessels took over. These were neither made nor owned on the island. As reported in the Guernsey Chamber of Commerce minutes of 1885: 'UK steamers left only about thirty shillings on a voyage whereas sailing ships left about forty pounds for harbour dues, provisions, etc'.[25] And later that decade the GCC minutes also noted: 'The value of the shipping property of the island... is now comparatively of almost insignificant proportions to what it was twenty years ago'.[26]

So, far less money remained on the island than in the earlier period of quarrying growth, but the arrival of steam, did bring many competitive benefits. Stone could be delivered to road builders on the mainland in a quarter of the time (ten hours in 1883) that sailing ships took, and the ships could carry far more rock. Steam also meant that the time-consuming handwork of reducing granite to acceptable sizes for macadamising could be replaced with steam-driven pulverising mills, which were built on the north side of St Sampson's Harbour.

Greater competitiveness, plus the good reputation of the Guernsey granite 'brand' itself, ensured the industry grew at an extraordinary rate. Exports rose from around 50,000 tons in 1852, to just over a quarter of a million tons in 1883 – a five-fold increase in only 25 years. A lot of this material came to London, where it was landed at Granite Wharf in Greenwich. This enormous increase in exportation had a consequence on the importance of the industry in employment terms. From being the seventh most important employer in 1851, this huge increase in export resulted in the quarrying and stone export industry becoming the second largest employer after agriculture by 1881.

What on earth was all this granite used for? In the early years of the century, those granite setts or cobbles were the material of choice for the streets of London. But they quickly lost their popularity. The hard-wearing Bordeaux Diorite led to shiny surfaces and that meant horses slipping on a regular basis. And the noise! Homeowners in London complained bitterly about the sounds of carts and horses rumbling over the granite surfaces. Also the wear and tear on the setts led to clouds of dust hovering over the streets of London, causing breathing problems, and necessitating the daily passing of water carts to hose down the pollution. No wonder that the biggest competitor to granite setts were wooden blocks!

Walking around London today, you can still see the impact of the island's material on the look of the city. Kerb stones made from granite can be seen everywhere – and still in very good condition.

We also know from the Mowlem company records, that the boom in railway construction during Victorian times used granite ballast for supporting the rails. Granite setts were also widely used in London as pathways for the horse-drawn trams that dominated public transport in this era. And the island's stone was also still popular amongst architects who used it to add gravitas to their buildings.

Episode Four: The Late Boom 1880-1913

By 1882, John Mowlem's company, now run by his nephew George Burt, had at least nine quarries in Guernsey according to company ledgers. They were situated either to the north of St Sampson's excavating Bordeaux Diorite or just south of the harbour quarrying the tough St Peter Port Gabbro.

After up to 50 years of quarrying, these sites were now deep in the ground. To bring the rock to the surface, horse-drawn carts at the quarry bottom were loaded and lifted by either steam cranes or what were called 'Blondins' (a sort of ropeway that enabled materials to be raised – named after the famous tightrope walker). At the surface they would be attached to cart horses, who would bring them to the processing mills situated around St Sampson's Harbour where, by 1914, Mowlem's had four crushing mills. Here, the rocks or 'spalls' would be broken by steam hammers or shaped by hand.

Pity the poor local householders, who according to GF Harris' notes, in his 1888 book on granite, had to put up with: 'an incessant din created by the noise of the hammers, chisels and crowbars of the workmen'.[27] And we should not forget the accompanying occasional noisy blasts of dynamite, for shattering rock, or gunpowder, for easing out big solid blocks for shaping.

This cacophonous, dusty, industrial scene was completed by the whooshing of the many windmills dotted across the landscape, used to pump out the groundwater, against which the quarry owners fought a constant battle. What a scene! And adding to the machine-made noise, we should include the shouts and chatter in French, of the many male and female stone workers, because at the start of 1880, immigrants from France were the largest group in an industry which employed nearly 2,000 workers.

1880 is also the moment that the rock-exporting industry made an important transition from sail to steam. In 1887, 88 steamers loaded at St Sampson's, alongside 665 smaller sailing ships. The steamships were vastly more efficient at transporting the processed granite, carrying up to 1,200 tons of material each, compared to under 100 tons on typical Guernsey built sailing-vessels.

The steamship revolution quickly ate into the cargoes of the local sailing ships. In 1893, steamships moved 237,000 tons of rock, compared to 93,000 tons by sail. And just three years later, steamships accounted for 363,000 tons and sailing ships just 63,000 tons.

Those 88 steamships that docked back in 1887, became an avalanche of iron clads by the turn of the century, with more than 2,000 of them loading in St Sampson's, compared to just 563 sailing vessels. And this steam-driven revolution off-shore was mirrored on-shore with the Mowlem company installing its first 'great' steam-driven crushing machine in 1882.

There were of course some downsides to steam. The iron ships were neither built on the island nor owned by Guernseymen. Steam effectively killed the local shipbuilding industry, and although freight costs were considerably reduced by the big, new fast ironclads, the Guernsey Chamber of Commerce in 1885, notes: 'most of the benefit usually derived from this our principal export has this year been lost to the island'.[28] All the profits for transporting the granite went to the mainland and into the pockets of the English owners.

Our Chamber of Commerce writer notes in his 1888 submission: 'The value of the shipping property of the island ... is now comparatively of almost insignificant proportions to what it was twenty years ago'.[29]

The beneficial impact of steam on efficiency however, came at just the right time for the island, as the booming UK construction industry was attracting new suppliers. Our friend at the Chamber of Commerce talks in 1883, about 'battling the Belgian stone' and 'even dressed stone coming from Norway'. Despite these worries, he was also able to boast in the same report: 'Guernsey's granite was now allowed to be superior to every other kind of stone for road making ... Their granite for road making purposes was admitted to be the best in the world, as was proved by the public trial on Blackfriars Bridge'.[30]

It seems that many customers in the UK agreed with this assessment, as the amount of granite exported in this late boom period, between 1880 and 1913, rose to extraordinary levels. The 1880 export volume amounted to a quarter of a million tons. But this was almost as nothing compared to the 1913 shipments which came to a truly astonishing 450,000 tons. Nearly half a million tons of rock blasted out of the ground, crushed, shaped and sent to provide the foundations for roads, rails, harbours, and public buildings. By 1891, quarrying had clearly become Guernsey's second business behind agriculture with 13.5% of the workforce engaged in the stone industry.

It took the quarrying industry nearly 100 years to reach this phenomenal peak in production, but sadly, it took a lot less time for the business to collapse. At the turn of the 20th century, we can already see a drop in the importance of the workforce, with 12.5% employed in quarrying. At the same time, the agricultural and horticultural sector was growing, to account for 35% of all males employed in the island.

Of course, some of this decrease in the workforce can be attributed to the growing mechanisation of the industry. And the investment in greater efficiency also reflected pressure on the Guernsey stone exporters from increasing competition.

A lucky fluke gave me the chance to learn more about the rivals to Guernsey for granite. By chance, I discovered that the Wellcome Foundation in London had scanned the annual reports of the medical officers from all the London boroughs. Fascinating to read, but also relevant to our understanding of the granite business, as these medical reports were the principal appendix to each London borough's annual Board of Works report.

Looking at two boroughs in particular, Wandsworth and Islington, we can derive from the 19th century some very 21st century marketing-style statistics. Starting with Wandsworth, this borough had immense road building or repair needs, as its population increased by 50% in the ten years from 1891 to 1901. In the Board of Works reports on road building from this decade and beyond, we see how Guernsey competed first with Cornish stone for contracts, then quarried stone from Enderby in Leicestershire, and finally from its sister island of Alderney. Guernsey dominated contracts in this borough for most of the period 1892–1912, with a share of contracts rising to 88% in 1905, only to then disappear as a supplier completely after 1909, when Alderney became the sole broken granite supplier to this part of London.

This domination of Guernsey as the go-to brand for granite, was also mirrored in another borough, Paddington, for which the Wellcome Foundation has data. Here, Guernsey supplied 90% of all granite used in this borough in 1900. What is interesting in this part of London is how many suppliers there were for granite – not only Alderney and Leicestershire, but also from Narborough in

Leicestershire, as well as Clee Hill, Aberdeen and even Quenast in France.

We can also learn a bit about the status of the Guernsey granite 'brand' through the eyes of the road building and repair procurers again from the Board of Works reports in the Borough of Clerkenwell. Here we can see how much they paid for granite from different sources. They bought Guernsey 'broken granite' at 17/1d per cubic yard, compared to rock from Leicestershire at 15/9d – so the island's granite had a price premium of 8% in 1894, and this premium rose to 15% in 1900. In Islington this premium was even greater. In 1892, Guernsey granite cost the borough's road repairers 17/6d per cubic yard, whilst Leicestershire granite could be obtained for only 12/10d. This meant there was a premium of 36% for the island's rock.

We must conclude from this window into cost prices that there was something about the island's granite that justified a significant price premium versus alternatives. It could well be that the reputation for its durability played a role in this price differentiation.

In 1907, the Metropolitan Borough of Wandsworth produced an annual report, which highlighted several interesting challenges Guernsey granite was beginning to face at the start of the 20th century. The 1907 report noted that 16,608 cubic yards of granite were purchased in 1906 – of which 53% came from Guernsey, 33% from Alderney, and 14% from Enderby in Leicestershire. The latter had recently had a railway line opened to the quarries, which made shipping granite south quicker and cheaper. This report also noted that the borough imported 1,274 linear feet of Norwegian kerb stone, and nearly as much Kentish pit flint as all the granite. Companies like Mowlem also faced local rivals for contracts for its Guernsey granite. In the 1906 accounts, the Wandsworth borough had six contracts with different island suppliers for its granite needs. So, Mowlem faced rivals not only from different countries but also from several local quarry owners.

This challenge to Guernsey's domination triggered a reaction led, not surprisingly, by the industry innovators – the John Mowlem company. Looking at documents now housed in the London Metropolitan Archives, there seemed to have been a slew of company quarry closures in Guernsey at the beginning of the century.[31] One closed in 1905, another in 1911, and four in 1914. In the company's annual reports, now housed in the Institute of Civil Engineers, there were some further tantalising hints of change. In the Mowlem minute book for 1913, two enigmatic statements appear: 'The question of surplus spalls at Guernsey was mentioned and it was agreed that the only method of reducing output was to stop Juas quarry' and 'In favour of Mr Wilson for effecting the sale in Guernsey of Baubigny and the Mills quarries'.[32] (They were sold to the Guernsey Waterworks company).

So, it looks like Mowlem had too many Guernsey quarries, and found that buying material from other quarry owners could work out cheaper. In addition, despite the very unemotional language used in the minute book, an interesting argument was recorded on 10 November 1913, with the following recommendation being made by some of the directors: 'Steps be at once taken to treat their Guernsey granite with a bituminous mixture because all authorities are now taking them up and discontinuing the use of plain granite'.[33] This viewpoint was not accepted by George Burt (John Mowlem's wife's nephew and managing director), who disagreed saying he: 'did not consider the output of Guernsey granite was being affected'. George Burt was wrong. As early as 1869, asphalt replaced granite setts on Threadneedle Street in London. It was quieter, and later, with the arrival of motor cars with pneumatic tyres, became a far more attractive road surface than dusty, noisy granite setts. As the internal combustion engine gradually replaced the 100,000 horses trotting through London every day in Victoria's time, so too it replaced the horse-drawn tram, and killed the need for granite-sett beds for the tram rails.

New technology in road building was not the only threat to the quarrying industry. We saw earlier the downturn in numbers of stone workers at the beginning of the 20th century. Why was this?

For many years, the quarry workers had worked in a sort of gig economy. Many of them were fishermen, who came ashore in winter and worked in the quarries, blasting out spalls which were transported and held in the mills until spring, when workers would appear to crush them.

These workers began to build greenhouses towards the end of the 19th and start of the 20th centuries. At first, they would put up one 100-foot vinery and then save to erect a second. The first vinery would be worked part-time by the man and probably full time by his wife. Once the second vinery had been erected, the combination of the two was enough to provide a decent living and as a result, many quarrymen gave up their rock excavating occupations. Let's face it, which would you choose: working on piece rate for little pay, in dusty, dangerous quarries, or tending grapes and tomatoes in warm, weather-protected glasshouses? No wonder the stone trade was starting to lose workers.

So as Britain and the Channel Islands entered World War 1, the hundred-year-old quarrying for granite business was facing several big challenges. First, more competition from other granite sources, both in the UK and abroad. Second, the arrival of new road-building technologies, which would dilute the demand for road metal. And thirdly, the attractive alternative for workers to control their financial destinies by building and cultivating profitable grapes and tomato vines.

Episode Five: The Decline 1918-1939

Although the signs of decline were apparent before the war, after the soldiers returned the need to work the quarries declined even faster. The alternative of tomato growing was too attractive. But the need to save up for that extra greenhouse resulted in many quarries relying on part-time workers, who found it more profitable to spend their summers working in the family vinery.

We can learn a lot about the years after the war through the increasingly active discussions about the island in the Mowlem minutes books. Here in September 1918, is the first sign that the world of Guernsey quarrying was changing: 'The question of reducing output from the Company's quarries in Guernsey was considered'.[34] This became even more pointed, a year later, in May 1919:

> The question of the disposal of the Company's property and interests in Guernsey was considered and the Secretary was authorised to make some tentative enquiries as to the possibility of effecting a sale.

But perhaps the strongest warning for Guernsey's biggest exporter came in the minutes of a meeting held in May 1923, where it was noted that the company had acquired the patents for the 'Blackstone' process for coating roads with tar or bitumen. At the same meeting, the directors also discussed forming a cement supply company for the marketing of Belgian cement.

So, it was clear that the Mowlem company was not disposing of Guernsey assets because they were going bust. It was because their business was booming and no longer needed to rely on the low value quarrying of rock when they could use faster, more profitable raw materials or technologies.

This became obvious in the Mowlem minutes of an April 1925 meeting, when Eric Burt reported back on a fact-finding trip to the island. His exasperation with the low profitability of their quarrying business resulted in him ordering that: 'a statement be prepared showing as nearly as possible the cost of production based on one week's work'. You don't do this unless you're unhappy with the figures. And the following year the minute book reports that the company were: 'interviewing the directors of the Guernsey Electric company (with a view to) obtaining a reduction in their charges for current'.[35]

Since the end of the 19th century, Mowlem had supplemented production of their own material by sub-contracting local firms to provide extra stone. After the war, the minute book shows the company either cancelling contracts, or reducing quantities with sub-contractors like the Fallas and the Corbets. In addition, they were closing their own quarries and reducing the numbers of workers in the crushing mills at St Sampson's. They also went a step further in 1927, by reducing the wages of the workers by 10%. By the way, in that same meeting in 1927, the minute book records that the company would be buying two new Rolls Royces for the directors!

Things reached a head in 1928, when the minute book boldly states: 'It was decided to tell all concerned that they should try to find other employment... since the board's decision to close down'.[36]

Finally, the end of Mowlem in Guernsey came in 1929, when they accepted an offer from the Fallas, to buy the crushing plant and stock. This was not an indication that the whole of Mowlem was suffering, as can be seen from this note from the AGM of 1929: 'A large quantity of road construction, maintenance and similar work has been carried out during the year and despite severe competition remunerative contracts in these branches are still being obtained'.[37]

The problem was not Mowlem. The problem was Guernsey. The Victorian era of municipal architecture and road enhancement was over. Road-building technology had changed. The great period of railway and tram expansion had finished. The UK's infrastructure was now so good, that granite from afar could be easily accessed. Competition from lower cost labour countries was increasing – particularly kerbstones from Norway. More mechanisation meant fewer people were needed. And finally, the horticulture industry was now booming, drawing more and more ex-quarrymen to its easier, more profitable lifestyle.

By 1935, there were only 310 people left in an industry that had employed many times more 50 years earlier. Nevertheless, Fenn and Yeoman[38] note that in the 1930s, there were still 268 working quarries and during that decade, exports of around 100,000 tones a year were achieved, with a slight peak just before World War 2, as the UK built runways ready for the impending fight against Hitler.

Episode Six: Local Recovery 1945-Present Day

The Occupation of the islands by Germans forces during World War 2 brought a sinister revival for the industry. Hitler was determined to make the island an impregnable fortress, and that meant stone construction. Some of Mowlem's quarries were brought back into production, resuscitating old engines, until spare parts could no longer be found.

After the war, the number of quarries continued to decline and by the 1960s only two remained, employing just 76 workers. And as of 1984, there remained just one quarry – Ronez at Les Vardes in the northwest of the island, which continues to extract up to 150,000 tonnes a year for local consumption, but with a plan to close sometime in the 2020s.

Why just for local consumption? After all, the demand for quality granite continues to exist, and quarry men throughout Europe continue to burrow into the earth's crust to extract rock. The reasons are probably multiple, but that stretch of sea between the island and the UK that was so useful in the early 19th century, now represented a barrier to trade, adding freight costs greater than its competitors.

So, there we are, another industry that grew, expanded, dominated and then declined. An industry created from natural resources, helped by sea transportation, exploited by a small group of entrepreneurial outsiders and locals, and then killed by changing technology and competition. But like a phoenix, Guernsey rose from the ashes of the quarrying industry and developed another island brand that was to become familiar to every household in Great Britain.

5: Who Killed the Guernsey Tom?

I was a bit stunned. Sitting back in my chair, listening to the wind whistling around the tower of the renovated church that now holds Guernsey's Island Archives. I had just spent three days reading the Guernsey Growers Association (GGA) reviews and annual reports, from its first edition in 1894, up to the latest in 2014. And it was like reading a Greek tragedy. A story about the birth, life and death of the Guernsey tomato industry.

There were of course epic heroes at the beginning. People who planted the first rows of tomatoes in greenhouses full of grape vines. Mr Poat who saved the infant industry from early death by bringing soil steaming and sterilisation from the USA to Guernsey. The Guernsey Tomato Marketing Board (GTMB),

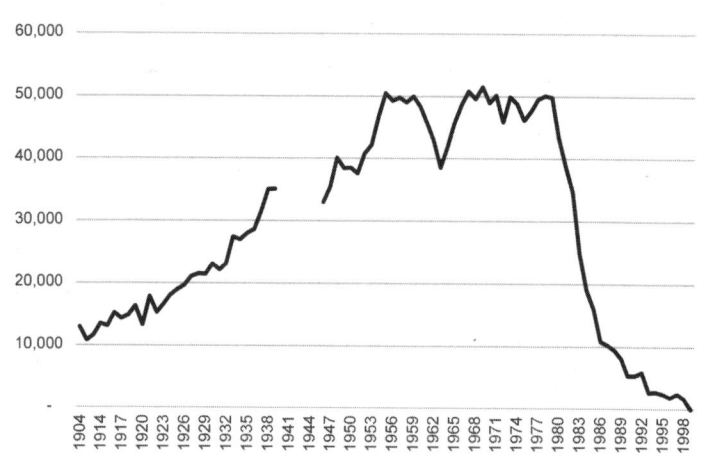

Fig 4: Tomato Exports (tons), 1912–2001.
(See Appendix for sources)

who coordinated the export of Guernsey Toms. And of course, the intelligent advice handed out by the GGA.

But there were also villains. Dockers who went on strike in 1972 and caused the destruction of millions of rotting fruit. The States, who limited expansion of vineries, rejected early demands for an experimental station, and arrived far too late with financial support for glasshouse modernisation. The EU and the admission of Spain, with its huge horticultural business. And throughout the Guernsey Tomato industry's 100-year history, the ever-present spectre of Dutch competition.

I looked through the couple of hundred 5x3 cards I had filled with facts and figures on the industry and tried to understand how and why an island industry, that had been such an important part of British culinary life, had died.

So, this is the story of the death of the Guernsey Tom and who killed it. I wanted to find the answer. Not just out of curiosity, but hopefully to learn some lessons that the Guernsey people might consider, as they move uncertainly into the future. Getting this answer won't be easy, and to do so, we need to start by going back into history and the origins of the growing business.

Why Tomatoes?

It seems probable that tomatoes originated in Peru and were first domesticated by the Aztecs in Mesoamerica (between Mexico and northern Costa Rica) around 500BC. It's likely that Christopher Columbus was the first European to see a tomato on his second voyage of discovery, but it was Hernán Cortés who first brought back its seed to Europe. And it appears that tomatoes began to be grown in Spain as early as the 1540s. These original tomatoes were the size of today's cherry versions, but yellow in colour – hence the original name *pomo d'oro*.

Their cultivation gradually spread to the rest of southern Europe and arrived in England around 1597, but here they were considered poisonous. This was mainly due to John Gerard, whose treatise *The Herball* in 1597, claimed the plant was poisonous and believed it to be 'of ranke and stinking savour', offering 'very little nourishment to the body, and the same naught and corrupt'.[1]

It was suggested that the acidic nature of the fruit, when eaten off the pewter plates of the time, leached some of the lead out of the material, causing a poisonous reaction. This was later debunked as 'tomatoes aren't acid enough, pewter dishes were never common enough, and lead poisoning accumulates too slowly to be linked to a specific meal'.[2]

Despite Gerard's warning, the tomato started to be used in English cooking from the mid 18th century onwards, and before the end of that century, the *Encyclopædia Britannica* stated the tomato was 'in daily use in soups, broths, and as a garnish'.[3] In the very first printed recipe for tomatoes, Maria Rundell's 1806 book *New System of Domestic Cookery*, she included directions for tomato sauce, tomato ketchup, stewed tomatoes and preserved tomatoes. This focus on cooking tomatoes was emphasised in the 1822 book *Encyclopaedia of Gardening*[4] where the fruit was described as good for sauces and soups, but mentions nothing about eating raw tomatoes.

Bit by bit, the tomato entered the consciousness of the British public. Even Mrs Beeton included a recipe for stewed tomatoes, which she called 'a delicious accompaniment' and Charles Dickens's wife Catherine, published a recipe for tomatoes in her 1852 tome *What Shall We Have for Dinner?*[5]

By the end of the 19th century, the tomato was pretty much established in the cooking repertoire of British housewives, and the demand for this fruit no doubt began to nag away in the minds of Guernsey entrepreneurs. But this nagging required something else to trigger the birth of the Guernsey Tom.

5: Who Killed The Guernsey Tom?

Greenhouses

The concept of artificially nurturing crops is not a recent one. Many authorities cite the Romans as the first practical users of the idea. Pliny refers to Emperor Tiberius in 30 AD being advised to eat, every day, something often wrongly referred to as a cucumber – in fact the correct translation of Pliny's remarks is the snake melon or Armenian cucumber. To satisfy Tiberius, his servants developed a sort of wheeled cart containing Armenian cucumber plants, which were warmed in winter by a covering of selenite or gypsum. This was transparent enough to let in sunlight, but retained the resultant warmth.

Proper glasshouses were first created by the Koreans in the 1450s, and eventually found their way to Europe. First in Holland, and then in the 16th century to the UK, when orangeries became the in-thing for the aristocracy of the time. The first reference to such a building in English literature came in the book *The Gardeners Labyrinth* written by Thomas Hill and published in 1577.

As often happens, the rest of the population were prevented from copying their 'betters' by the imposition of both the window tax in 1696, and the glass tax in 1746. Fortunately, the Industrial Revolution led to the creation of techniques for manufacturing cheap glass, and these taxes were revoked in 1696 (window tax), and 1848 (glass tax). This release from extra costs, opened the flood gates to the golden age of Victorian glass houses for the wealthy upper classes. Many examples still exist today from this period, including the three wonderful heated greenhouses of Charles Darwin in his garden in Down House, and the world-renowned example in Kew Gardens.

And what about Guernsey? It seems that the first heated and glazed greenhouse on the island was built by Peter Mourant, in what is today Candie Gardens. This was in 1792 and it is still there today – just! Apparently, it was originally designed to grow pineapples. Of course, this posh structure, built to enable an eighteenth-century hostess to show off exotic produce at her soirées, has not much to do with the tomato industry, apart from providing the first visible inspiration for some early Guernsey horticulturalists.

So, the two key actors in the future industry were now available on the island but what triggered the next step in the story? Like many innovations, the Guernsey greenhouse full of tomato vines was the child of many different cultural strands, which I'll now try to unpick.

The Protection Instinct

Guernsey residents were very much aware of the benefit of protecting crops from the potential harmful effects of nature. Since the 16th century, Guernsey had extensive apple orchards which were used to make cider. The William Gardner map of 1787, suggests that about 7.5% of the island was covered by orchards[6] – quite a bit more than the 6% of the island inhabited by greenhouses in the 20th century.

Now what you don't want with apple trees, especially in the spring, are strong winds to blow away the blossom, and according to the Guernsey meteorological office, most years there are only five or so days of calm weather on the island. So, to protect vulnerable trees, the Guernsey farmers in the north and west, would surround their orchards with tamarisk hedges, which grew well in low lying salty soil, and cut down the harmful tendencies of the cold easterlies. Further south, the same protective inclinations resulted in the building of high banks topped with furze and elm hedges, which can still be seen today.

Making the Best of Poor Land

At the start of the 1800s, Guernsey was not making the best use of its land, with only about 50% being used,[7] and the methods for growing crops were pretty poor. So, it is highly likely that agriculture was not adequately supporting the population of 16,000 people.

Early greenhouses were most often to be found in the north and west of the island, where a lot of the land was substandard – not the best place for crops or grazing. And so, the small holders in these areas had nothing to lose by experimenting with different methods of farming. William Garner's map supports this view, as do a couple of contemporary writers. Quayle in 1815 wrote: 'The proportion of land lying waste is too great'[8] and in 1834 Inglis noted, 'large tracts of the north and west are but imperfectly reclaimed; and present a very uninviting and sterile appearance'.[9]

The Financial Instinct

Staying on this theme of the land in the north and west of the island, we can also note that these were the areas where the most Guernsey fishermen and quarry workers were to be found. Both professions were not well paid, and often impacted by the weather, the seasons, or consumer demand.

This meant they had to think of additional ways to supplement their wages. And a greenhouse turned out to be a pretty good solution. Inside the protected glass cocoon, quite a lot of fruit and vegetables could be grown and sold, for decent money, locally. Of course, both professions had day jobs so greenhouse crops had to look after themselves for much of the day, and in these low-lying areas the high water-table meant roots could find moisture easily. No doubt in the early days of the 19th century, these small holders experimented with many different greenhouse crops. Most quickly settled on grapes as a crop that delivered a pretty good return. That's why, by the way, Guernsey greenhouses are called 'vineries'.

The Export Instinct

Guernsey may be an island, but since the 1500s, the locals have looked outward for their economy. First, it was woollen stockings exported mainly to Paris, and later to the UK. Then came surplus cider, not drunk by the locals. It was noted in a Directory of the Islands in 1874, that 'the cider of the island is of excellent quality and hundreds of hogsheads are annually shipped to England'.[10] Even tobacco was shipped abroad, until its export was banned by the Privy Council for interfering with production in the American colonies.

Clearly, the inhabitants of Guernsey had an eye for markets outside the island and no doubt the produce from the early greenhouses was already being lined up for potential sale abroad. They were able to see and feel the Gulf Stream, giving Guernsey an earlier wake-up call from winter than on the mainland, providing them with a distinct advantage over their horticultural rivals in the UK.

Getting it There

It was all very well exporting knitwear, cider and tobacco, after all they were fairly tolerant of long sea journeys, but if you wanted to export perishable horticultural products, then you needed something quicker and more reliable, than the sailing ships that frequented the English-Channel during the pre-Napoleonic era.

The arrival of steamships changed everything. More reliable

than sail, faster as well. The two regular services that started from Guernsey to Southampton in 1824, gave an opening for our early greenhouse pioneers. And when this service was augmented by the building of the Southampton to London railway line in 1840, suddenly growers had access to the produce markets of the world's biggest booming Victorian city.

The Five Factors That Changed the Face of the Island.

At the start of the 19th century, these five intertwined threads came together to kick start the infant horticultural industry. But the Guernsey Tom was at first preceded by another fruit — the grape. From little lean-to vineries mainly in the north, grapes were first exported to Covent Garden in 1830; three tons arriving in 1855; four tons a year later; 50 tons in 1876; 600 in 1885; and 2,500 tons in 1915.[11]

There is a nice quote from Jacob in 1830, which shows (perhaps with a little exaggeration) the extent to which greenhouses were changing the look of the island:

> Perhaps there is no spot of ground in Europe of the same size, where there are more greenhouses or hothouses than Guernsey, there being scarcely a gentleman's house without one or more and many of the tradesmen have their graperies.[12]

The Greenhouse Boom Arrives.

The success of the early greenhouse pioneers and their grape exports, encouraged more small holders to think about doing the same, especially in the north, where we know the poor soils didn't encourage other forms of agriculture. But they still had to build their vineries. And here came a first stroke of luck. In the

Vale parish there were lots of quarrymen who had a perk. They could take away misshapen bits of granite that were not considered viable by their bosses. These could be used to create the low walls on which glass frames could be constructed. So, they had the first ingredient needed to make a proper greenhouse rather than just a lean-to, but they still needed to put a frame on their granite bases. Unfortunately, they just didn't have the time or carpentry skills to do this.

As luck would have it, along the east coast of Guernsey were a string of shipbuilding yards that were going out of business. Set up to build wooden sailing ships in the post Napoleonic boom time; the new technology of iron-hulled steamships demanded an infrastructure that was beyond the capabilities of the yards facing the Little Russel. This meant there were many ship's carpenters scratching around looking for new ways to earn an income.

Well guess what? If you squint your eyes, look at an old Guernsey greenhouse from the 19th century; the 30 x 9 metre wooden structure resembles an inverted ship's hull. And so, yet again, Guernsey's industrial history reflected the smooth movement from one set of skills to another – ship's carpenters helping quarrymen to build a new horticultural industry, quickly and cheaply.

Paying for the Greenhouses

It wasn't just shipbuilding that morphed into the greenhouse business. The Guernsey century of privateering and smuggling, which came to an end after the Napoleonic Wars had left a very useful legacy. Lots of money. And this was now put to use funding an expansion of horticulture. This culminated in a transformation of the island landscape, which can clearly be seen in the first Ordnance Survey map of the island in 1898.

Many of the vineries were unheated 30 x 9 metre houses, that were built at a cost of around £100 (£10,000 at 2023 prices), half of which was provided by the banks – using perhaps some of that privateering booty slushing around the island. Indeed, in his article on the Guernsey Grape Industry, Peter Girard noted: 'It seems quite obvious that a large amount of capital was available for investment in the island, and it appears that the local banks were generous with the loans which they issued'.[13]

Who Were the Early Pioneers?

Our early horticulturalists were mostly part-timers. Quarrymen using their misshapen granite. Ship's carpenters, reinvesting their wages from building other people's greenhouses in their own vineries. And fishermen around Bordeaux Harbour, Grand Havre, and along the west coast, supplementing their seasonal income. The preponderance of glass structures in the north and west is obvious looking at the 1898 Ordnance Survey map, and reflects the tendency of our three types of pioneers to be based in this part of the island.

Yes, But What About Tomatoes?

At some point in the 1860s, some unknown genius on the island had an insight, which went something like this: Hmm, I've got this grapevine that comes into my greenhouse through a hole in the wall, and the fruiting tendrils hang from supports strung across the top of my vinery, but the soil in the glasshouse isn't being used. Why don't I plant something in the bare earth – that way I can double my production without increasing the space? This idea of double use was not new to Guernsey. In 1830, Jacob noted that: 'Most of the orchards are cultivated, having garden vegetables under the trees'.[14] The idea of using the soil under the grape vines was the aha! moment for the Guernsey Tom. Tomatoes had arrived in Guernsey around about 1834, and we know that at some point before 1865, Frederick de Jersey at La Corbinerie, Oberlands, had his gardener JH Parsons, plant some tomato seeds he probably got through his connections with the Spanish wine trade. Once ripe, the tomatoes were taken by Parsons to the market in St Peter Port, where he sold ... none. The tomato was clearly still a slightly worrying fruit for most Guernsey cooks.[15]

Nevertheless, between the 1860s and 1880s, the idea of eating tomatoes began to take off, and in 1884 Mr J Poat at Richmond, produced the first main crop under glass in Guernsey. These were sold locally, with the honour for the first tomato exporter to the UK going to James de Garis in 1888.[16] His initiative was quickly copied by all those ex-quarrymen, ship's carpenters and fishermen in the north who realised that the mild Guernsey climate meant tomatoes could be grown and shipped to the mainland much earlier than their horticultural rivals in England.

Early toms meant premium prices and lots of profit. That's why 'CR' noted, if rather over the top, in 1893 'every cottage has its glasshouse'.[17] And it wasn't just Guernsey residents who wanted a piece of the action. Between 1871 and 1901, just under 6,300 people from England and Scotland migrated to the island – a lot of whom were horticulturalists.

They came with money and big plans. They were not interested in lean-to, unheated vineries. They came with the intention of building batches of 12 metre wide spans – and heated, using anthracite, imported from Wales, to warm water pipes that helped force tomato plants to earlier and earlier fruiting.

For these immigrants the cost of land was important, and the cheapest acres were in the north, which had the additional benefit of being closer to the coal-importing port of St Sampson's. Moving coal by horse and cart was an expensive business, and undoubtedly kept back greenhouse development on the southern plateau and west coast.[18]

An Early Set Back

The early insight that crops could be grown under the grape vines on the unused vinery soil was a great idea, until the growers began to see their plants becoming diseased, the result of direct planting in the soil. The Guernsey Chamber of Commerce remarked in their annual report: 'considerable amount of disease in the tomato crop. In fact, it is estimated the loss was quite 15% of the crop'.[19]

In effect, the Victorians, in their efforts to produce bigger and more abundant fruiting plants, had bred out most of the plant's natural defensive genes, according to Roger Chetelat at the Tomato Genetics Resource Centre in the University of California.[20]

The first solution to overcoming the problems of diseased soil was pragmatic. Bring in fresh soil from somewhere else. Rob Batiste in July 2022's *Guernsey Press* noted: 'Growers bought fields sometimes several miles from their vineries, removing the topsoil and transporting it to their holdings'.[21] This was an expensive solution for the famously parsimonious Guernsey grower.

Fortunately, yet another of those innovation heroes came along. Remember Mr Poat? The first grower to plant a tomato main crop. Family member, William, was the hero of the hour. During a trip to America, he came across soil steam sterilisation. On his return to the island in 1902, he found through experimentation of baking soil in his Mum's oven that steaming the soil killed the diseases, and tomato plants flourished in the resulting sterilised soil.

As Mr T Renouf remarked in the GGA 1955 review: 'It is doubtful whether the tomato industry of Guernsey would have survived if the steaming of soil had not come to the rescue of growers'.[22] This discovery led to portable soil steamers becoming a familiar sight around the island in the winter months.

The First Boom for Tomatoes

Mr Poat had saved the infant tomato industry and as a result, between 1902, and the start of World War 1, exports to the UK boomed. In 1904, the UK imported just under 54,000 tons of tomatoes, with Guernsey Toms accounting for around a quarter, produced by 300 or so growers. And by 1913, Guernsey tomato exports amounted to 12,000 tons, putting the 2,000 tons of grapes shipped to the UK that year in the shade.

It may have been the first boom, but it still touched only a proportion of the British population. Many were still hesitant about this fruit, considered only fifty years earlier as poisonous. In a lovely little book called *The Book of the Tomato* in 1948, the author noted: 'Even as late as 1900 those who ate tomatoes were considered almost heroes or martyrs'. In the same book the writer emphasised the continuing strangeness of the fruit: 'Even books published just before the 1914 war almost treated the tomato as a medicine'.[23]

Shewell-Cooper also notes, though, that in a conversation, King George V: 'stated that he attributed the popularity of this fruit to the 1914–18 war, for during that period the munitions workers had been highly paid and as a result were able to buy tomatoes in large quantities and so learned to like them'.

Growing Grows Up 1918-1933.

In AC Bescoby's book *Modern Horticulture* published in the early 1900s, he writes: 'The last decade has seen very considerable changes in the views of the world at large on the subject of horticulture. It was formerly a happy-go-lucky industry'. And indeed, we can imagine that was true in Guernsey. Innovation here took many forms — soil sterilisation for example, and moves from the rough-skinned fruit of the Victorian era to the smooth surfaces of the tomatoes we know today. Swift steamer transport took crops from the island to the markets of the UK, anthracite-fueled hot-water-heated greenhouses leading to early cropping, plus the heavy demand during the war from cash-rich munitions workers. All made it just seem so easy to make money.

But, after the war, things got more serious. Mr Poat's annual soil sterilisation innovation cost money. Transport from St Peter Port to Southampton cost money. Anthracite to heat the vineries cost money. And rail freight to the regions of the UK cost money. All these costs had serious impacts on the Guernsey grower. In an interview with Mr J Le Page back in 1970,[24] he suggested that in the 1880s, it was possible to make a good living out of one 30 x 9 metre house; by 1914 two such houses were necessary; and by 1933 three or four houses had become the economic norm for the average grower. This need to expand can clearly be seen in the 1933 Ordnance Survey map of the island, where the early growing nucleus in the north had become crowded with vineries, reflecting the benefits of economies of scale. But a close inspection of the mid-thirties survey map also shows that a new area of high-density greenhouses was apparent along the west coast, and in a small area up on the southern plateau.

All this extra glass, and a cohort of now around 700 growers (nearly double those around in 1914), enabled Guernsey to really ramp up its tomato exports to the UK, from around 17,000 tons in 1918, to over 27,000 tons at the time of the new map survey in 1933 — a whopping 59% increase.

Not all the increase in exports came from the building of new glass. By 1933, other factors began to play an important role. First, remember the benefits those early pioneers felt they had by siting themselves in the north? Where the water table was higher, and so enabled the grape or tomato vines to feed themselves? Well, by the 1920s, growers realised that this was actually a drawback, as the higher water table made the soil colder and retarded early fruiting. So, growing in pots began and ended the local link with the soil of the island.

Then there was the benefit of heating greenhouses. More heat meant earlier fruit and higher prices in the UK. And we can see an enormous increase in the use of anthracite in the period after World War 1. Imports rose from 32,000 tons in 1918, to over 106,000 tons in 1927[25] – a rise of well over 200%.

A third factor in increasing productivity was light. Those early houses, with their granite walled surrounds, limited light quite a bit, and so fairly quickly growers replaced the stone bases with more glass – up to 1.5 metres on the frontage. These three factors helped growers increase their yields dramatically. And in turn, this productivity enabled Guernsey to maintain an incredible 25% share of the total UK tomato imports.

So back in 1933, who had the other 75% of imports? Holland had about the same share as Guernsey with 25%, but it was the Canary Islands with a 44% share that really dominated the UK greengrocers – benefitting from its warmer climate, lower costs and earlier ripening. The *GGA Yearbook* for 1931 talks about competitors for the first time since the association was founded, and notes for 1930: 'this year we have been faced with abnormal competition from the Canary Islands'. This was something the island growers would have to get used to in the upcoming 60 years!

The worry about foreign competition came at the height of the Great Depression and, to help protect British interests, the Ministry of Agriculture and Fisheries imposed duties on imported tomatoes except 'those from Empire countries'.[26] These duties

5: WHO KILLED THE GUERNSEY TOM?

amounted to 2d per lb from 1 June to 31 July, and 1d from 1 August to 31 October.

Did it help? Probably not. Again, the GGA records note in 1934 for the Guernsey grape business that rival grapes grown in Belgium were 'not discouraged by the tariff of 3d per lb'. Also, Canary Island tomato imports were biggest from November through to April, when no duties were levied. So, the only real loser was the Dutch grower who cropped just a little later than Guernsey.

The *GGA Review* in 1930 also noted another competitor: 'The increase in tomato growing on the mainland has become a permanent menace to our prospects'. Worthing and the Lea Valley were particular flies in the ointment.

Of course, the GGA had reasons to big up the competitors – in reality, in 1939, 150,000 tons of tomatoes were imported into the UK plus around 75,000 tons grown at home. Sensibly, Guernsey fought back both against these homegrown tonnages, and the persistent threats from the Canary Islands and Holland, by focusing on quality and reliability. The island introduced inspection of fruit in 1934 and tomato grading in 1936.[27]

Just before World War 2, the island arrived at pretty much its maximum density of greenhouses. After 1945, only an additional 131 acres of new glass was erected. The red gold rush was pretty much over. Anyone who thought about growing was now doing it and earning a pretty good living. We will come back to this 1930s building boom later in our mystery story – 40 years later in fact. And it will provide a clue to who might have killed our Guernsey Tom.

World War 2

The tomato industry was centre stage when the Germans decided to invade the island. A sweep of Guernsey by German aircraft on 28 June 1940 identified a convoy of trucks at the harbour in St Peter Port. Assuming these were military vehicles, the Luftwaffe attacked and bombed 49 trucks, killing between 30 and 40 people. The trucks were in fact loaded with tomatoes waiting to be shipped to the UK.

German planes were back on 30 June, this time with troops and the occupation of the island began. Eventually up to 10,000 German troops were billeted on the island, plus another 10,000 prisoners of war. So, despite nearly half the Guernsey population of the island evacuating in June 1940, the island still had to support the food needs of around 40,000 people.

As you can imagine, many of the people who were evacuated were growers and their greenhouses were left empty. The States, in the guise of the Glasshouse Utilisation Board (GUB), took over their management. And under instruction from the island's German commandant, the GUB ordered growers to replace the mono crop of tomatoes with a range of vegetables including potatoes, beans, peas, cabbage, cauliflower, sweetcorn, parsnips and carrots.

Some of these crops grew pretty well, but the vineries never really succeeded with either potatoes or wheat, which meant that the Guernsey population had less food during the war than their sister island Jersey, who are still famous for their outdoor Jersey Royal potatoes.

Many of the greenhouses were required to either sell or give their crops to the Germans and a proportion of glasshouses were designated as growing crops solely for German consumption.

The five years of occupation may have changed what was grown in the greenhouses, but the structures remained very much

5: Who Killed The Guernsey Tom?

in use during the whole of World War 2, with just 100 acres lost to blast or shrapnel from the German anti-aircraft and coastal defence guns.

The Forties and Fifties

The horticulture industry bounced back quickly after the war, with 1948 being described by the GGA as a 'boom year' when exports hit 40,000 tons for the first time. And by 1955, the GGA memberships had increased from the pre-war level of just under 800 members to 1,270.

This 1955 membership figure represented the high water mark in the history of the GGA, and was also reflected in the export tonnage of tomatoes (50,500 tonnes), reaching a level to be seen again only twice (1967 and 1969). About 1,000 acres were under glass for tomato cultivation in that year, or 15% of the land, and it is estimated that around 5,000 people were employed either directly or indirectly in the growing industry.

During the late 50s, it seems the States panicked about this industry growth, and in 1956 put a three-year ban on any increase in the land under glass (a ban that was actually maintained until 1963). Their main concern seems to have been worries about water consumption. Between 1948–1954, consumption in the island had been 44 million gallons, 55% of which was attributable to the growing industry. They were also concerned that any further increases in acreage would necessitate the importation of outside labour, which would in turn lead to an increased domestic water consumption. The ban was actually quite beneficial, since it forced the industry to look at modernising existing structures, rather than just adding new ones to be used alongside aging vineries. It also turned out to be unnecessary, as modern irrigation techniques limited water usage.

We also can't ignore the States continued insistence on the application of the Glasshouse Control Law (1936) which issued permits for the erection of new glass, and limited expansion to an annual prescribed maximum. This was, at least in part, to maintain the beauty of the island at a time when British tourist visits to the island was growing.

The mid-50s also saw the creation of the Guernsey Tomato Marketing Board (1953), that was to establish itself as the commercial arm for the island's growers. In this period, they were selling the island's Guernsey Toms to UK greengrocers – a calm before the arrival of the supermarket storm.

Another innovation at the end of this period was the birth of the Horticulture Advisory Board in 1956, with their Experimental Station constructed at Longue Rue in St Martin's in 1961. This came just under 50 years after the GGA had made a presentation to the States requesting the creation of such a unit, and just under 100 years after the Dutch founded their world-famous agricultural college in Wageningen.

This date – 1955 – is a crucial one in our attempt to identify who killed the Guernsey Tom. It turns out to be the date when the industry should have turned and looked at itself with greater objectivity, because this was the year when the growth of the industry stopped. After 60 years of continual expansion, protected by tariffs, encouraged by growing consumer consumption, the industry should have looked to the future. Should have checked out how the Dutch were building technology advantages. Should have worried about the arrival of supermarkets. And should have made some brave and imaginative decisions about the shape of the industry moving forward. But it didn't. And even though exports carried on, around 50,000 tons a year for another quarter of a century, this flatness should have rung alarm bells on the island.

25 Years of Complacency

As with many industries across the UK, the 60s was a period of prosperity for Guernsey growers. The island was dominated by the Guernsey Tom, with one in four males and one in six females employed in a horticulture industry (approximately 5,275 full time equivalents) that generated 80% of the island's visible earnings.[28]

Bigger greenhouses, now consistently orientated east-west, were the future, with more glass and thinner frameworks, artificial irrigation systems, troughs of peat or straw for growing mediums, and better heavier-cropping varieties. This all enabled the more forward-looking grower to make a good living and buy a new car every year. Not really a surprise, given that the GGA noted in the period 1960–1970 cash return per acre increased from under £7,000 to over £12,000, with the new 60 centimetre glass generating 35% higher returns than the old pre-war 30 centimetre panes.

All these innovations were not taken up by most growers. By the mid-60s, something like 75% of tomato growers were over 40,[29] and many were more interested in today's profit rather than tomorrow's business.

Proof of this comes from the GGA Growers Conference of 1964 which indicated that, of the 1,150 acres of land under glass at that time, around 40% were houses built over 44 years ago, and only 30% were less than 13 years old. This old glass could not produce early or heavy crops and was beginning to demand more and more costly maintenance.

The following year (1965), the GGA ramped up its warnings by saying: 'the present labour situation, where for every two workers over 60, there is less than one under 20, does not give much hope for the future'.[30]

And to really press home their worries, in the *GGA Yearbook* for 1969 they wrote: 'Too many growers are relying on their fathers and Grandfather's glasshouse investments and some seem surprised to find they can barely make a living. What other industry could possibly survive on assets that are 40–50 years old?'[31]

Were the GGA being over the top with their concerns? The 60s were a real roller coaster ride in terms of exports, with some huge drops in output in 1962 and 1963, but then coming back with a massive harvest in 1967 of over 50,000 tons and an even bigger figure for 1969 of 51,502 tons.

The reality is that there were some huge storm clouds for the industry appearing on the horizon, and it seemed that very few people, apart from the GGA, took much notice of them.

So, what were these brooding cumuli-nimbi? Well, we have already heard from the GGA that the industry was relying on a lot of old and inefficient greenhouses. That was already worrying – especially as the States noted that modernisation of houses was happening only at the rate of 1% per year.

Then we have the Dutch. This well-established adversary was certainly not relying on old glass. Between 1957 and 1962, they increased glass houses by 1,750 acres. And in 1965, Hinton noted: 'The ability of the Dutch to penetrate our market so successfully is the result of economic and social factors which raise the Dutch glasshouse industry to a much greater level of efficiency compared to with that of our industry as a whole'.[32]

And reinforcing this point, the GGA in 1968 remarked that 'unlike the Dutch we failed to take advantage of the opportunity to modernise in the fifties while the protective duties remained secure'.[33] The Guernsey growers' nemesis in fact increased its exports of tomatoes from 130,813 tons in 1958, to 226,000 tonnes in 1964. That's nearly double in only six years.

If that wasn't enough of a looming storm, there were others as well. The cosy relationship with greengrocers was changing. In 1963, these shops handled 87% of fruit and veg sold in the UK, with only 3% coming from the new-style supermarkets. But by 1968, just five years later, these new outlets had just under 20% of fresh vegetable sales and were growing at dramatic rates.

The Tescos *et al* of the times were far less forgiving of the little Guernsey grower and his careless picking, haphazard packing and indifferent management. Here was a customer who wouldn't let anybody get away with anything.

Growers were also beginning to have problems with production costs. New artificial growing mediums such as peat or hay-filled troughs cost money, as did CO_2 enrichment. And marketing to persuade those supermarket shoppers to buy Guernsey Toms cost money. In 1967, the GTMB had a budget of £60,000 for advertising (£770,000 at today's prices) which the growers had to pay for.

And even though the benefits of increased output from modern metal-framed 60 centimetre glass was obvious, the costs were becoming harder and harder to absorb. In the mid-60s the cost of a new house was around £20 per square foot, compared to £2 back in 1903. Wages for labour nearly doubled between 1953 and 1970, fuel actually did double and fertilisers increased by 80%. Set against all this, in the 60s, annual prices achieved by the GTMB only rose in the decade by 20%.

To sum it all up, at the end of the 60s, there were four potential threats to the tomato industry: old inefficient greenhouses; dangerously forward-looking Dutch growers; difficult and demanding supermarkets; and increasingly hard to recover cost increases. But it must still be said that the 60s were a great time to be a grower, as Terry Howard notes: '(The 60s) was a fantastic time to be working in the industry. Growers were making profits; new cars were being ordered on a single year's profit from half-acre vineries'.[34] So, the stage is now set for the final bloody chapter in the Guernsey Tom story.

The Death of an Industry

I personally came across the Guernsey Tomato industry in 1970, as a young Geography student writing a thesis on glasshouse locations in the island. I spent a wonderful summer cycling around the lanes, interviewing over 60 growers, and drinking about the same number of cups of tea. I also had an incredibly lucky experience, knocking on the door of a big vinery in the north of the island where I met Colonel Harry Poat. At the time, I didn't realise he was related to the famous Poat, who'd saved the industry with his knowledge of soil sterilisation. Colonel Poat was distinguished in his own right from his exploits in the SAS, and he gave me the benefits of his family's experience growing tomatoes. I was also able to poke around the old ledgers of eight vineries, where I uncovered tons of arcane information on freight costs, anthracite prices and just about everything related to running a tomato vinery in the 20th century.

Back when I was writing my thesis, the tomato growing business had just reached 80 years old. It had been producing around 50,000 tonnes of fruit per year for export to the UK since the end of the 1950s. A stable industry employing around 25% of the Guernsey workforce, and looking forward to being the island's preeminent employer for the foreseeable future. And yet in the space of 30 years, this cornerstone of Guernsey's economy disappeared, with the last 'Toms' exported in 1999.

So, who killed the Guernsey Tom? There are many potential culprits: the favourite suspect is probably the Dutch growing industry with the backing of their government; then there is the EU with its admission in 1972 of Spain and Portugal and their huge horticultural industry; closer to home, there are some that say the States played a key role in the 'Toms' demise; and, perhaps more provocatively, one might point the finger at the Guernsey growers themselves.

But first let's paint a quick picture of the last 30 years of the tomato industry. Despite all sorts of mutterings about the effect of joining the EEC as it was then known, our new relationship with the continent in 1973 didn't really have any immediate effect and, once in, the mutterings sort of stopped. The 1970s were a continuation of a plateauing of export volumes that lasted pretty much a quarter of a century from 1955 to 1979, with the volumes of tomatoes consistently around 50,000 tonnes a year, apart from a drop during six years from 1960 to 1966.

There were storm clouds lurking just over the horizon during the 70s. These rather ominous-looking clouds seemed to have been a combination of outside pushes, that upset the greenhouse equilibrium, and pulls that enticed growers and their families into a new direction. First then the pushes.

Government Legislation

The Guernsey tomato industry had been protected at certain times of the year by UK tariffs. They placed an extra cost for competitors from overseas who tried to sell during the peak exporting season for Guernsey. As noted in the GGA Annual Report of 1985: 'For fifty years we lived in a protected UK market'.[35] This protection came to an end as a result of negotiations that enabled the UK to join the EEC. It was not however instantaneous. The tariffs were gradually phased out over the 70s, and finally only disappeared in 1978. Its effect was to make Holland more competitive – the last thing that Guernsey growers needed, as their nemesis had been a thorn in their side for decades. More of that later.

It has often been said that the Guernsey islander cherishes his and her independence, and doesn't take kindly to interference, especially from Parliament or the States. They were however more than happy to accept the cocoon that the UK government gave them with the tariffs. They were less inclined to be positive about other laws imposed on them. For example, between 1957 and 1962, the States imposed a moratorium on extending the area under glass. As noted earlier, this was partly to try to preserve water supplies, but also to ensure the island remained as attractive as possible for tourists. This restriction obviously limited the size of the industry and made Guernsey less competitive.

The States did try to help the industry as well. They created a loan scheme enabling growers to modernise their vineries. Unfortunately, it wasn't very effective, and so was replaced with another scheme, designed to train youngsters through a glasshouse renting scheme.[36] Truth be told these youngsters were increasingly disinclined to join the growing industry, whatever incentives were provided, as can be witnessed in 1970 when the States Advisory and Finance Committee noted that 84% of all school leavers with A-levels left the island.[37]

The generally lukewarm support by the States for the tomato growers may have reflected the local government hedging its bets. The *GGA Yearbook* of 1978, looking back at the early 70s, noted that the States aimed to 'stabilise the size of the industry at 850 acres, maintain the volume of tomatoes to avoid a reduction in scale and encourage the development of profitable flower production'.

So, flowers were one answer for the States. Another was electronics. The arrival on the island of Tektronix, the American oscilloscope maker, with its modern management techniques, clean working environment and profit-sharing, created equipment for the new electronics age. The Billet of 1971 clearly foresaw a contraction of tomato growing, and believed the Tektronix experience could be the way for the future.[38] That Billet failed to mention the finance sector, which in 1971, had already attracted something close to 40 banks to the island!

5: Who Killed The Guernsey Tom?

It is interesting that the States could see a contraction of tomato growing as far back as 1971, even though exports remained close to 50,000 tonnes a year until 1980. They chose not to really do anything proactive to prevent this decline happening. Why? Well, it looks like they had a couple of other options up their sleeves. We've mentioned Tektronix and the arrival of the electronics age to the island. We've also seen how flowers as an alternative crop in greenhouses offered advantages (more on this later). The finance industry looked promising, and last but not least, tourism was still growing and becoming a serious force within the island.

The Economics of Tomato Growing

If a laissez-faire attitude by the States, allied to a loss of tariff protection, was the first push factor that impacted tomato growing, the second was just the sheer cost of greenhouse cultivation of tomatoes. You could imagine the States members being assaulted by numbers that clearly, were going to make the Guernsey Tom an expensive fruit in the future.

The first cost was heating fuel. Guernsey growers needed oil to warm up their vineries to force their crop to ripen earlier and facilitate higher consumer prices. But in 1973/74 the Middle Eastern countries began punishing the West for supporting Israel in the Yom Kippur war and, in the winter of 1973, oil doubled in price. The impact on growers was huge. From paying 1.24 pence per litre for gas oil in 1971, they had to find 4.07 pence per litre in 1975, and 13.5 pence per litre in 1980.[39] This was an increase of close to 1000% in ten years.

Now against this fuel increase, it's important to point out that Guernsey's latitude meant it used 30% less fuel per acre than the Dutch and 20% less than growers in the south of England. Our Guernsey growers also responded to the fuel increases, reducing by half their consumption through lower temperature requirements and earlier sowing dates.[40] Nevertheless, by the end of the 70s, fuel represented at least 30% of a growers' costs.[41]

How do you save on fuel? Let the sun do more of the work. The trouble in Guernsey was that as an early pioneer of greenhouse cropping of tomatoes, many of their ageing vineries used small panes of glass, thick wooden frames, and often relatively high granite wall bases. All these elements reduced the penetration of the sun's rays. And in Guernsey at the start of the 70s, more than half of the greenhouses were more than 60 years old, or as stated in a Billet of 1974, 'nearly 50% of (vineries) had become technically obsolete'.[42]

The solution was bigger panes of glass, thinner aluminium frames and no granite wall bases. Two problems with this at the time. Knocking down an old vinery to build something more efficient would mean a short-term loss of income. And putting a better greenhouse on new land was almost impossible due to States planning laws. Even if the grower could handle a temporary profit hit or find some available land, the cost of borrowing money in the 70s was almost prohibitive. Going to the bank for the money to put up an efficient new greenhouse in 1970 would cost a grower 7% in interest, 11.25% in 1975 and 17% in 1979.

For the small grower these interest rates were prohibitive. And local banks were pretty reluctant to advance money to these small growers for several reasons. They saw that Eastern European tomato growers, with their lower labour costs, were pushing their way into the big German market which in turn led the Dutch to replace sales to their Teutonic neighbours, with an increase in exports to the UK. The Dutch were helped by the strong pound at the start of the 70s, and again at the end of the 70s, which made tomato imports from the Continent much more attractive than fruit from Guernsey.

The banks also saw how the removal of tariffs would impact Guernsey volumes. And they were right. After the final tariffs were eliminated in 1978, Dutch exports to the UK market rose from 20,000 tonnes in 1977 to 56,000 tonnes in 1980. A rise of over 250%!

As the *Billet* of 1974 predicted:

The majority of small growers face great difficulty in justifying capital to renovate. The capital cost of creating and equipping small areas of glass is disproportionately large and the small scale of operations does not earn sufficient income to provide a living.[43]

Guernsey could have modernised. But it would have needed to be done in the 1950s and 1960s, when tariff protection and low interest rates made it a much more doable project. Nevertheless, the industry carried on throughout the 70s, maintaining output at a high level thanks to technological innovations. And at the same time, many small growers clearly had had enough, and decided to leave the industry, or turn to less difficult flower cultivation. There were 1,107 of them in 1978, but only 708 in 1980.[44] For those remaining 700 growers, little did they know they were living on borrowed time. The Dutch were coming!

Holland - Guernsey's Biggest Export Competitor

An article by PF Bailey in the *GGA Review* of 1959, puts it this way: 'I am very worried about the increasing import of tomatoes from Holland'.[45] And a year later, in 1960, the GGA reported on a visit to the Dutch Tomato growing area: 'The whole marketing system is incredibly slick and swift. From the moment the fruit is picked, the whole emphasis is on speed of handling. The result is attractive and almost plant fresh fruit in the greengrocers of Europe. That is our challenge'.[46] As early as 1958, the GGA was telling its members about the Dutch Advisory Service, which provided an advisory officer for every 100 growers (in the UK at the time there was one for every 200 growers).

The Dutch Advisory Service was backed by the University of Wageningen, called in 2020 by *The Guardian*: 'The nucleus of the Dutch (food) innovation juggernaut'.[47] In the same article, *The Guardian* writer points out that the small country of Holland is 'consistently among the world's top food exporting nations and the world's second largest exporter of tomatoes and onions'. Today, Holland is the number one tomato cultivating country by yield, producing an incredible 144,352 tonnes per square mile.

Summing up the importance of Wageningen, Berkers and Geel in an article on the transformation of the Dutch growing industry between 1930 and 1980, noted the following:

> Research organisations, especially the well-known agricultural University of Wageningen, played a central role by actively participating in the development and implementation of many radical technological innovations related to the construction and functioning of greenhouses, providing the sector with a strong knowledge base regarding process technology.[48]

By the way, the Dutch founded Wageningen in 1876. Guernsey didn't agree until 1961 to open its own Experimental Station. Despite this focus by the Dutch on research and development, the GGA in 1965 describes their continental tomato growing rival as follows: 'The Dutch grower (our chief competitor), whose only advantage over us is cheaper fuel, puts in more effective effort and achieves more economy than does the typical Guernsey grower'.[49] This idea that the Dutch competition is purely down to heating bills, is just not the whole story. In 1965, the gas field discovered around Groningen had only just begun to be used, and was unlikely to have really impacted costs. Later in the 70s, it did play a big role, thanks to the Dutch government subsidising fuel costs for many years after the EU had told them to stop.

With such a small land area, the Dutch saw greenhouse production as a very efficient way to use their small areas of land in a highly profitable way. Dutch greenhouse acreage doubled between 1955 and 1965, and in turn trebled its production of tomatoes.

Initially, the Dutch steered clear of the UK and its combination of home-grown tomatoes and those imported from Guernsey in the peak summer season. Instead, they focused more on Germany (in 1957, 72% of Holland's crop went there), but as sterling became stronger in the 70s, and as tariffs were gradually phased out, the Dutch piled into the UK. Their sales soared and by 1980, they had taken 28% of the market. No wonder the greenhouse acreage in the Netherlands continued to expand in the 80s at a rate of 500 acres per year.[50]

So, whereas in the 1950s Guernsey was just a 'bit worried' about Dutch growers, by the end of the 70s, they were scared stiff. Guernsey had become an unenviable rock between two hard places – Spanish crops early and late in the season, and Dutch toms in the middle.

Hang On, What About the Consumer?

It may seem extraordinary, but after reading nearly 100 years of *GGA Yearbooks*, the first mention of the consumer of tomatoes didn't come until 1968. Ultimately these shoppers were the people who broke the growers' backs, starting in the 1980s, and delivering the final *coup de grâce* in 1999. So why did they turn against their Guernsey Tom?

First, we need to blame the growers, whose declining income in the 70s led them to reduce marketing expenditure on their brand by the GTMB. This resulted in a decline in loyalty to the Guernsey Tom and opened the door to interlopers like the Dutch.

We can also blame the growers for not listening to consumers and their changing salad preferences. RG Kimber puts it this way back in a GGA article in 1982: 'To make a salad you (used to) require lettuce, tomatoes and cucumber'.[51] And in the same article it was noted: 'The humble salad which used to be part of the Sunday tea or picnic is not only much more versatile nowadays, but also commonplace all year round and highly cosmopolitan'.[52]

The Dutch did listen, and began growing beefsteak tomatoes for hamburgers, plus peppers, for adding colour, texture and flavour. Baby tomatoes followed. British supermarkets became allies of the consumer, prioritising good value, consistent quality and freshness. These demands became increasingly difficult for the island's growers to meet.

But speaking of the tomato consumer, how did it happen that the British became such fans of this little red fruit? To find out, I decided to investigate their appearance in cookery books since the beginning of the 19th century, and used the immense collection of recipe books at the London Guild Hall Library as my source.

The first book I found was the 1831 *The Cook's Oracle*, which had just one tomato recipe out of a tome holding over 1,000 recipes. By 1845, Francatelli's *The Modern Cook: A Practical Guide to the Culinary Art* already shared 34 tomato dishes out of 1,268 recipes. Things went back a bit with Eliza Acton's famous *Modern Cooking for Private Families* with only seven options from over 1,300 recipes.

Mrs Beeton seemed to have been a fan, as can be seen in this extract from her book:

Tomato, or Love Apple an admirable sauce by itself, it enters largely into a great number of our best and most wholesome sauces. It also may be cooked and brought to the table like other vegetables, in several different ways; or eaten raw cut into slices like cucumber, but much thicker, and dressed with salt and pepper, oil and vinegar in the same way.[53]

That sounds familiar, doesn't it? Oh, and she also wrote a book on garden management that included tips on cultivating tomatoes.

At the turn of the century (1900), Matilda Lees Dods' *Handbook of Practical Cookery* again had a poor coverage of tomato dishes with just twelve choices out of 639. After World War 1, Elizabeth Craig's *Family Cooking* provided 29 recipes.

It looks like World War 2 and the need to 'grow your own' really nurtured the appreciation of the tomato plant, with sixteen recipes from *A Kitchen Goes to War*, out of just 150 options. Elizabeth David continued this elevation of the tomato's stock by featuring 46 recipes in her hugely influential *French Provincial Cooking* (1960). And finally, the sainted Delia Smith in her *Illustrated Cooking Course* (1989) had 26 recipes out of a total of 1,036.

A Lot of 'Pushes' for Guernsey Growers

The Guernsey growers struggled through the 1970s, maintaining their tonnages, but doing so with a reduced acreage, and far fewer operators. Income dropped as competition from the EU, particularly the innovative Dutch, began to bite. And opportunities to become more efficient, like their Dutch competitors, were hampered by very high interest rates on investment in better glasshouses, a difficulty of acquiring sites, and a general lack of interest from banks for loans. As if that were not enough, every month growers got bills through their letterboxes for fuel which must have had many of them, metaphorically, reaching for a pistol.

These 'pushes' to force the industry to decide what it wanted to do were joined by the States who not only appeared to see a grim future for growers, but could identify a very clear Plan B and possible Plan C, with tourism potentially becoming the new economic driver and, later, finance.

The Pulls

The first pull was really close to home. If tomatoes take a lot of heat and water to bring them to ripeness, what could growers cultivate that uses less of these two cost centres? The answer was flowers – more specifically freesias and carnations.

A second pull was tourism. Why work seven days a week, watering, picking, sorting, when you could run a guest house and have most of the day to yourself? More importantly, it provided a source of occupation for the grown-up children of growers. Just as the 80s saw tomato volumes in freefall, the same decade saw tourism become Guernsey's most important economic sector, with nearly half a million visitors coming to the island in 1989.

And a third pull was the burgeoning finance industry. It overtook tourism in 1983, as Guernsey's leading money earner and by 1989, 70 banks had offices in the island. Banks required a lot of people – ideally local people. A nice office, regular hours, weekends off – a lot to attract young people instead of taking over from Mum and Dad in the greenhouse.

A final pull came from the pressure of a population that had grown by 7,000 in the 20 years from 1971 to 1991. Guernsey needed more housing. And low profit-earning, land-hogging vineries were just ripe for conversion into estates for finance workers. Why soldier on when you could sell up to a property developer and retire?

The Year it All Went Wrong.

Our look at the pulls and pushes that shook the tomato industry acted as a pressure cooker on the island's number one exporter. Something had to give, and it seems that 1979 was that moment. As the GGA put it, looking back from 1986: '1979 was the crucial year that changed everything'.[54] We don't see that in the export tonnages for this crunch year. Guernsey still managed to grow and send to the UK just under 50,000 tonnes – pretty much at the same level as most years in that decade. What we do see is a year in which growers made 'very modest or nil profit'.[55] You could imagine a lot of growers around the Christmas table in 1979 saying: 'That's it, I've had enough'.

Battered by fuel increases, hammered by cheaper competitors, shunned by the banks, many growers did indeed say, that's enough! 575 acres of glass were used for tomato growing in the crunch year of 1979. Four years later in 1983, that figure had dropped to 250 acres. A fall of just over half. We also see this loss in acreage very clearly in the export figures:[56]

- 1980 43,368 tonnes – 13%
- 1981 38,808 tonnes – 10%
- 1982 34,673 tonnes – 11%
- 1983 24,846 tonnes – 28%

Some growers just left the industry, others carried on but now growing less fuel hungry freesias and carnations. But the decline in area devoted to tomatoes kept on dropping. In 1986 only around 100 acres remained for cropping the red fruit. And that was the year the Guernsey Tomato Marketing Board, for so long the protector of fruit quality and champion of the Guernsey Tom brand, announced on 10 October 1986: 'The GMTB will cease to exist as such from the end of October'.[57]

In the 11 years from 1979 to 1990, tomato growing, the once dominant social and economic force on the island, shrank by just under 90%. A few growers soldiered on but in 1999 the industry died – as the *GGA Yearbook* put it: 'Exports of round tomatoes ceased for the first time since World War 2'.[58] In the same article, the writer noted: 'As a percentage of what is termed export sectors to the economy, horticulture's contribution in 1973 was 36%, today it is 4%. In the same period finance has grown from 11% to 60%'.[59]

Did the Guernsey Tom's Death Really Matter?

I am not impartial when trying to answer this question. My brother-in-law's family had a vinery that we used to visit when my kids were young. I loved that unique smell, when the greenhouse door was opened, to let the nippers in to pick some fruit for lunch. I cherish the memory of a summer writing my thesis, cycling round the island, interviewing growers and spotting those first-generation granite and wood-framed glass structures. And as a marketer, I am proud that Guernsey created a truly great consumer brand.

Today it's just so sad to see marooned sagging vineries being suffocated with bindweed, brambles and bushes. Too expensive to pull down, they just sit there, unloved and unwanted. But they do represent a living lesson for the island. The thriving Dutch tomato industry shows the Guernsey Tom brand perhaps need not have died. Listening more closely to consumers and the supermarkets, investing earlier in research and development, having greater political will and leadership on modernisation, could all have helped. Let's see, over the following two chapters, if the lessons we can learn from the downfall of the Guernsey Tom have been taken up by our next two Guernsey brands.

6: Buckets, Spades & Windbreaks

There are approximately half a million islands in the world. And for many of us, they seem to have a magical effect on our imaginations. We dream of being Robinson Crusoe or maybe Tom Hanks in the film *Castaway*. We imagine ourselves beachcombing, sitting under palm trees or digging for buried treasure. Islands just seem to open a door in our heads. You could say that eventually we all catch the disease of 'islomania'.[1] We all just seem to love islands.

Guernsey fits quite well into this island obsession. It is small enough to get around quite easily. It has more than 20 sandy bays to enjoy, impressive cliffs that require steady nerves to circumnavigate and an interior of well-tended, hedge-protected fields which are more like well-tended gardens than agricultural plots. Its perimeter is spiked with long fingers of wave-lashed rock, many decorated with ancient, and not so old, fortifications.

And for the keen botanist, Guernsey's flora is extraordinarily varied, not only because of its mild climate, but also for its propensity to attract shipwrecks. It is these maritime misfortunes that explains the profusion of plants native to South Africa and the Canary Islands that can be found along the coastline and in people's gardens. The first of a duo of South African escapees is the Sour Fig, a low-lying succulent found rambling all over the coastal areas, and its compatriot, the scarlet-flowered Guernsey Lily, despite its name, also from South Africa. The import I love the best though is the *Echium Pininana*, a towering mauve plant that gazes imperiously at the passing tourist and originates from the Canary Islands. There are of course, a profusion of British flowers as well. They colour the banks on either side of the island's country lanes, thanks to an edict which prohibits farmers from trimming hedges until after the wildflowers have seeded.

Not only is the island littered with accidental germinations from exotic locations, but the landscape is also a sort of historical dustbin of archaeological delights – from Neolithic tombs to Roman galleons, Civil War fortifications, smugglers' hideaways, pirates' cellars, Georgian town houses, Victorian extravaganzas and Nazi obsessions. No wonder Guernsey has a tourist industry: so much for the islomaniac to discover and enjoy.

I'll divide this chapter into four parts: the early days of discovery as a destination, the middle years of growing popularity, the era of waning interest and finally the small but intriguing rebirth. Throughout these four sections, I will consider the key needs of the potential visitor to the island: how much will it cost; how will I get there; where can I sleep; and what can I do there?

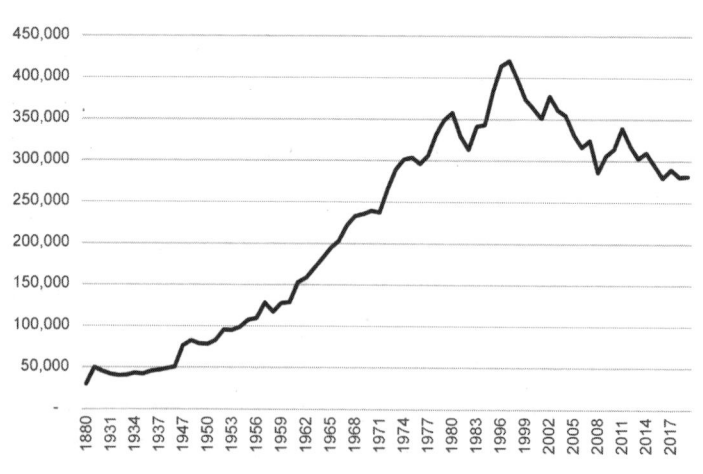

Fig 5: Tourist Arrivals, 1880–2019.
(See Appendix for sources)

6: Buckets, Spades & Windbreaks

The Early Years

Marketing people often say that to get people to do anything, they first must be made aware of what is available. In Guernsey's case, we can probably say that the first injection of knowledge about Guernsey for the British public came at the end of the Napoleonic Wars. 4,000 British militia had been billeted on the island to protect it from the French, and in 1815 these soldiers returned home and spread the word about this beautiful little island jewel. Some of them decided to stay and live out retirement on their pensions in the island, where the cost of living was considerably less than the mainland, as noted by one visitor to the island in 1838: 'Here, too, house-rent is less than in England, and no taxes'.[2]

These retirees in turn, were visited by friends and family, who acted as early ambassadors for the nascent tourist business of the island.

This growth in awareness of Guernsey as a potential holiday destination can be seen very clearly in the Google Ngram Viewer,[3] which cleverly scans books published since 1600. Using this tool, I plotted the number of mentions of 'Guernsey' and 'holidays'. The Ngram Viewer shows an upward trend of mentions, from as early as 1760, with leaps in the 1840s, the 1860s and then a steady growth into the 1900s. The use of the island as the hero of Victor Hugo's book *The Toilers of the Sea* probably didn't do any harm either – inspiring Renoir to visit and paint 18 pictures, mostly of the cliffs around Moulin Huet on the south coast.

In addition to books featuring the island, magazine articles grew steadily in profusion throughout the Victorian era. And finally, it's important not to forget that Queen Victoria herself, visited the island twice – in 1846 and 1859 – her visits no doubt adding to the British public's interest in the island.

So, Guernsey found itself increasingly mentioned in books, magazines and by word of mouth from family and visitors of retired military men. Once enticed, potential tourists needed to get to the island. The first regular mail service to Guernsey started in 1794, and at that time the crossing was made by sailing vessels and therefore dependent on wind and currents. There is a reference to a lady in 1800, making the crossing and taking two weeks to get to the island;[4] and in 1821, a crossing by a certain Mr Walmesley to Jersey from Southampton, took 41 hours going and 70 hours coming back![5]

No wonder Ansted notes in 1862: 'The dread of a rough passage is so general that many persons are deterred from visiting the Channel Islands'.[6] The very best that a tourist could hope for was a crossing of around 36 hours.[7]

The first steamer service started in 1823, and travel got easier with the rapid construction of railway lines to the ports of Weymouth, Poole, Southampton and Plymouth. The historian Jonathan Duncan, notes in his 1841 book on the island, that the journey to Guernsey from London via Southampton, took 15 hours.[8] And even as late as 1873, a letter from Sir David Weddersburn indicated that his paddle steamer from Southampton left at 8.30pm and arrived in St Helier only 12 hours later.[9]

Not only did the crossings become quicker, but cheaper as well, thanks to the growth in competition for journeys across the Channel. In 1862, the Brighton Railway got the right to operate steamers to the Channel Islands, sailing from Littlehampton. The Southwest Steam Navigation Company started in 1845, from Southampton to the islands, and were followed by the Weymouth and Channel Islands Steam Packet Company in 1857, who sailed from Weymouth (the shortest route to Guernsey). They were bought by the Great Western Railway company in 1888, who together with the London and Southwestern Company dominated the cross-Channel routes. It should be noted that, even though the steamer services made the journey to the island easier, when these boats arrived in Guernsey, they had to anchor off St Peter Port, and have their passengers disembark using small tenders (as do passengers on cruise ships today). Not very comfortable or easy, especially in choppy seas. This was resolved in 1864, with a harbour extension, which meant the UK steamers could use a berth at the White Rock.

Transport improvements made Guernsey accessible. But what sort of people began visiting the island? It was certainly not the lower or even middle classes, for whom the idea of a holiday was Sunday. The 1871 Bank Holiday Act did give workers a few paid holidays a year – not enough though to open up Guernsey as a holiday destination for most UK families. It was only the wealthy who had the time and money to visit the island, and particularly, curious moneyed people.

In the 19th century, the fashion for the curious to go on the Grand Tour continued, now made much easier and safer thanks to the arrival of rail transport (and from 1840 the expertise of the Thomas Cook company). Most upper-class young men and women went off to visit Europe. These trips were following well-established itineraries and so offered no real surprises for the more curious minded.

This is where Guernsey provided something different. Close to the mainland, but very French, and still underdeveloped compared to the booming industrial revolution in the UK. Here an amateur botanist, occasional archaeologist, keen bird spotter or even aficionado of sea bathing could really enjoy their hobby. And their pockets benefited as many items for sale were not taxed, and the exchange rate between Guernsey and the mainland was very favourable.

It is likely that the first tourists to come to the island were wealthy, privileged upper-class adventurers who wanted to experience new things, and take home tales to share with their circles of friends. People like Sir David Wedderburn who wrote about his visit to the Channel Islands in the spring of 1873.[10] He stayed at the Old Government House Hotel, which had been converted to a high-quality residence in the 1850s. The search for a bed for the night was of course high on the agenda for visitors to the island. At the time of Sir David's visit, the *Hill's Directory* of 1874 identifies ten hotels, four smaller hotels and 119 lodging houses (more on this later), mostly in St Peter Port.[11]

Wedderburn spent his time walking, participating in organised excursions and meeting prominent people of Guernsey society. He visited Sark and Jersey, both of which were more advanced than Guernsey in their embracing of the new tourist industry. His trips around Guernsey were in horse-drawn charabancs or what he called 'waggonettes'. He noted many shops were already catering to the needs of visitors to the island, and had become handy stopping places for refreshments around the island. These were to become the foundations for future country hotels.

This visit by a titled lord in the third quarter of the 19th century reveals that what he did 150 years ago is precisely what the modern visitor to the island still does today! The words of Renoir in 1883, could easily be echoed by a visitor in the 21st century: 'What a pretty little place! What pretty paths! Superb cliffs, beaches such as Robinson Crusoe must have had on his island!'[12]

There was also, though, a less attractive side to the island for the Victorian tourist, one that again could easily be words spoken by a modern-day holiday maker. This from an Irish visitor in 1846: 'Picnics and quadrille parties ... are the general, almost the only, amusements; for, in the matter of amusement, it must be allowed that Guernsey is in a state of great stagnation'.[13] This grumpy complaint was by no means unique. A decade earlier, the author of an article in the *United Services Magazine* made a similar complaint: 'Trade is very dull; there is no enterprise: the shops are very poor affairs; and every other thing seems on the slenderest scale; there is, in short, no life, no bustle. Not an amusement going on'.[14]

Even worse for Guernsey, our Irish visitor makes the ultimate damning criticism of this emerging holiday destination:

> Almost all visitors cut short their stay in Guernsey, and hurry off to Jersey, where, if society is inferior in refinement (a matter of comparative indifference to the migratory tourist), there are, at least, facilities for killing time which the more aristocratic island does not afford.[15]

This indifference to the needs of the tourist will emerge time and again throughout the 200 years of holiday-making on the island. Hold that thought – we will come back to it later.

We have been describing visitors to the island after the Napoleonic Wars, but just how many are we talking about? The first indication of a real tourist industry comes in the AGM of the Guernsey Chamber of Commerce in 1869, when they note: 'Another source of prosperity now existed in the attraction which the island presented to strangers'.[16] The same article refers also to '(the numbers of) visitors had greatly increased'. And in the Chamber of Commerce's 1876 AGM, they note: 'During the past summer the number of visitors to the island has been immense'.[17]

The first real figure was uncovered by John Uttley in his book on the Channel Islands, published in 1966.[18] He indicates that in the 1880s, the number of combined English and French visitors was around 30,000 a year. This interest in the island can also be seen in the leap in the number of guidebooks about Guernsey in the 1880s. The five decades preceding 1880 had seen about two guidebooks a year being published, but in the 1880s, 14 books appeared, reinforced by large numbers of magazine articles about the island as well.[19]

By the eve of World War 1 in 1913, the number of visitors had risen to 50,000[20] – quite a figure given that the island itself only had 40,000 inhabitants. And to accommodate them there were approximately 17 hotels[21] plus many lodging houses.

So that was the Victorian period of Guernsey's tourist industry. A time when the adventurous and well-heeled upper classes visited the island to enjoy the peace and quiet, visit ancient monuments and indulge in a little amateur archaeology. Perhaps they emulated Renoir and dashed off a water colour or two, or enjoyed a ride out to the north or west coast in a horse-drawn wagonette to socialise with the locals. Guernsey was being put on the tourist map and would benefit from these early pioneers after World War 1.

The Arrival of Mass Tourism

The next figure on tourists visiting the island comes in 1930, when the number of visitors was estimated at 45,000[22] – about the same figure as 1913. So, after World War 1, people returned to the island for holidays but with no real growth in numbers.

There may well have been a change though in the class composition of these visitors. As we have seen, Guernsey visitors in the Victorian era were primarily from the upper classes – people who were financially independent. After World War 1, trade union membership grew quite quickly and these bodies were increasingly able to negotiate holidays with pay for their workers. For example, in 1918, the Print Union was able to get one week's paid holidays for all their members and, by 1925, it is estimated that 1.5 million manual workers had paid holidays.[23] They joined their salaried managers, many of whom had enjoyed vacation privileges for decades.

A growing number of these less-privileged workers began visiting the island. To accommodate them, our 17 hotels dotted across the island in 1913 had grown to 21 establishments by 1934 and to 31 by 1939,[24] helped by the change from horse-drawn to motorised transport, which meant the outlying parishes could benefit as much as St Peter Port in this new tourist industry.

The biggest trigger for tourist growth came in 1938, with the passing of the Holidays With Pay Act that gave the right for all UK employees to one week's holiday per year. This brought the number of manual workers with holiday pay up to ten million, and even though this may have offered the potential for many more visitors to come to Guernsey, it was not yet the reality. At the outbreak of war in 1939, tourist numbers were still stuck at around 45,000 per year, which is amazing considering that, in the same year, Jersey's tourist numbers reached 200,000. The other island of course faced south and claimed more sunshine each year. It also seemed more willing to invest in hotels, boarding houses and even holiday camps.

One could surmise that the tomato industry provided a more attractive option for the average Guernsey person than dealing with tourists. The cost of building a greenhouse was lower than extending your home into a guesthouse. And for the generations of locals who had worked the land; cultivating crops under glass was not as much of a mental stretch compared with pampering to demanding visitors. And the States seemed keen on preserving an agricultural island look, rather than 'polluting' the countryside with tourist amenities.

Of course, tourist growth was taken out of the hands of the Bailiwick in 1940, when 1,000s of visitors from the Continent arrived in the unwelcome form of the Nazis.

After recovery from the German Occupation, 1950 was the real lauchpad for the island's mass tourist industry. Like a rocket, the visitor numbers from this date rose each year at an incredible rate, only coming to a halt in 1989 – a pretty fantastic run of 39 years of growth. From a total of 51,087 arrivals in 1946[25] (nothing compared to Jersey's figure of 224,000), the number in 1989 amounted to 460,000[26] – a growth of 800%! These 40 years were Guernsey's moment in the sun as a seaside holiday destination.

We should pause here and talk about one of the main reasons why Guernsey enjoyed this period of success. The sun. The Channel Islands are the most southerly part of the UK. Spring arrives four weeks earlier here than on the mainland, the island gets around 2,000 hours of sunshine a year[27] and tops sunny spots like Bognor on the south coast of England. For mainland workers, perhaps working all day in a factory or commuting in crowded trains, the thought of a week or two in the sun must have been very appealing. No wonder the States of Guernsey Tourist Committee used the slogan 'The Sunshine Island' in their advertising during the 30s, 40s and 50s. And there is even a case of estate agents getting in on the act, with this copy in a sales leaflet for the sale of a house called La Marcherie at Icart: 'Guernsey holds the sunshine record in the British Isles and Channel Isles for 34 consecutive years'.[28]

Sunshine may well have been a major driver for visitors to the island, but it was not the only one. What changed after the war? Awareness of the island was helped by the Channel Island's status as the only British territory occupied by the Germans. The prospect of cheap booze, fags and tax free shopping may have been another factor.

Ultimately, it's likely that British government legislation was the main provocation for people to go to Guernsey on holiday. World War 2 had left the UK in deepest debt and currency reserves were practically gone, so, foreign exchange restrictions were placed on the population. With not enough foreign money to pop over to France or Italy for a seaside vacation, the British, especially those in the south, turned to the islands of Guernsey and Jersey where their pounds were welcome.

Another intriguing attraction to the island has been proposed. In 1947, the Transport Act created British Rail, an organisation with, at that time, 655,000 employees. These workers were not paid excessive wages but, as Richards & Mackenzie note in their book *The Railway Station*: 'Wages were not lavish, but they were supplemented officially by company provision of domestic fuel, uniforms and later free railway travel'.[29] The key is the last perk – free railway travel. Now you may say yes, but that only got them to the coast for free. However, British Rail took over the old railway companies that sailed ships to the Channel Islands. So, any of the 600,000 BR employees could potentially get to Guernsey for free! You can imagine that, especially for those living in the southern part of the UK, this was a really good deal. Potentially, visitor numbers and awareness levels were boosted by this major UK employer – whose work force numbered over 800,000 people by 1953.[30] Even as late as 2002, this perk was mentioned in an article by Simon Vermeulen in the Guernsey Chamber of Commerce monthly magazine *Contact*: 'Loss of assisted passages to Sealink employees, the major carrier at the time, which alone accounted for 10,000 foot passengers'.[31]

The Channel Island ferries didn't have it all their own way. In 1939, the current airport site was opened for business with four grass runways. It was a miracle that it happened, as public opinion was dead set against this new modern form of transport and many were concerned at the significant loss of agricultural land. Indeed, the go-ahead was given only by the smallest of margins in the States (26 votes to 25).

1939 turned out to be a bad moment to open an airport, as one of its earliest visitors was the Luftwaffe. Normal service was resumed in 1946 and in 1974, the airport passed a significant milestone – the La Villiaze site saw half a million passengers pass through its terminal building.[32]

By 1960, the trickle of visitors after the war had reached well over 100,000 a year, and most of them were ordinary workers enjoying their week's paid holiday. They came by train to the ports of Weymouth and Poole, and then disgorged onto the British Rail passenger steamships.

Where were they to stay? Not in posh hotels on the front in St Peter Port. This was the boom period for guest houses on the island – initially converted private houses with a few extra bedrooms, but eventually new-builds, specifically designed as reasonably priced accommodation for families with children.

The actual amount of accommodation created in the 50s and 60s is pretty mind boggling. From the tiny base of 17 hotels in 1913, by 1967 the island had 12,600 registered beds in 784 hotels/guest houses, and an additional 1,000 beds in self-catering establishments.[33]

And what did they do when they left their guest houses or hotels after breakfast each morning? Catching a bus to the beach was undoubtedly the first choice – armed with windbreaks, buckets, spades, bats and balls, sandwiches and thermos flasks. But although Guernsey occasionally topped the UK sunshine league, the weather and temperature could not be relied on, and so alternatives were sought – a mooch round the souvenir shops in town, a boat trip to Herm or Sark, or a visit to Saumarez Park. They could walk along the cliff paths, perhaps try a bit of fishing, or visit one of the annual shows or the Battle of Flowers, even drop in to the Odeon or Gaumont. Not a huge amount of choice, certainly in the 50s and early 60s. But we shouldn't forget these were early days for tourism and holiday makers were still enjoying just the simple pleasure of not going into work the next day.

By the end of the 60s, this narrow range of things to do on the island was even noted by the conservative IDC (Island Development Committee). In a 1967 Billet, they remark that there were limited facilities for tourists during wet weather, but feared that the cost of providing more amusements would be capital intensive and underutilised for large parts of the year.[34] The committee therefore accepted there would be only modest growth in visitor numbers, as they would not be able to offer much more in terms of entertainment. Their solution was to try to build up the off-season period.

This involvement by politicians in the tourist industry at the end of the 60s reflected the simple fact that visitors spent a lot of money on the island. In the Billet of 1971, it was reckoned that the tourist industry represented 25% of all export earnings – at a time when the equivalent in the UK was 5%. And the comparable figure for Spain was 5.5%, with even Barbados only at 14.5%. Jersey however outdid Guernsey with tourism, representing 39% in 1969.[35] No wonder the island commissioned the first ever Travel Survey at the start of the 70s (more on this later).

Mentioning Spain and Barbados is rather pertinent as Guernsey entered its third decade of significant tourist numbers. Remember our early adopters after World War 2 who started flocking to the island? By the 1970s, their children had left home, their income had consequently gone up and the idea of a bucket and spade holiday no longer seemed enough. They had done 'the sandwiches on a cold blustery beach' holiday. They now wanted more. They wanted guaranteed sun. They wanted warm swimming pools. They wanted exotic food. They wanted modern hotels with ensuite bathrooms and night-time entertainment. And they wanted it all to be taken care of by someone else. Yes, they wanted a package holiday to Spain!

This was the new competition for Guernsey and its tourist industry. The surprising thing is that it took so long for it to impact the numbers visiting the island. Package holidays started in the 60s, but they were eye-wateringly expensive. In 1964, a seven-night holiday in Malta cost £215, or the equivalent of £3,787 today. Costs for continental package holidays began to fall dramatically with the arrival of jets – reducing journey times. For example, a flight by jet to Mallorca in the mid 1960s was two hours and that is still the case today. So, an hour less than it took to sail on the British Rail ferry from Poole to Guernsey, and only an hour longer than flying from Heathrow to the island.

Cost also dropped. Jets were not only fast, but they were also big and offered increasing economies of scale. At the time that these planes were shuttling hordes of English sun-seekers to Mallorca or the Costa Brava, BEA and British United were still using turbo prop Viscounts or even World War 2 DC3s to bring visitors to the Channel Islands. And it's interesting to note, that despite the importance of tourism to the economy, the States resisted allowing jets to land until 1976.

And once our sun-worshippers arrived in Spain, they were whisked off to ultra-modern, multi-storey skyscrapers overlooking sandy beaches, with ensuite bathrooms, bidets and even, if they wanted, a full English breakfast. The Guernsey visitor was still confronted with old-fashioned guest houses or dusty hotels – and this despite the best efforts of the States, who recognised the danger of island accommodation being compared poorly with the Mediterranean competition. Laws were passed in 1966 to raise the standard of accommodation, which led to a decline in the number of lowest grade guest houses. Despite this reduction at the lower end of the spectrum, 1968 saw the total number of beds available in the island reach its all-time peak at 14,492 beds.[36] And during the 70s, three major new hotels were built – St Pierre Park, Novotel and La Grande Mare – the latter two on the West Coast. There was also an extension to the Duke of Richmond Hotel in St Peter Port.

Visitor numbers continued to rise throughout the 70s and 80s to fill these beds. So who were they? The first travel survey conducted in 1970 provided a definitive idea on who the island's holiday makers were.[37] 97% were from the UK, mostly from London and the south-east, and in the age group 35–64. They tended to be from the upper social classes. And just under 60% came by air – because it was quicker. Probably this could all have been guessed. But then come some more unusual statistics. Only 18% of visitors were families with children (in the UK, 35% of households were families with children) – maybe because getting to the island was too expensive? And in 1970, 54% had never visited Guernsey before – quite a high proportion of first timers.

The survey also asked the obvious question: why did you choose Guernsey for your holiday? Top of the list was the climate (24% indicated this), along with 'For a change' (24%). 'Peacefulness' came next (22%), and then 'recommendation from friends' (21%). When they were asked if they considered Guernsey 'unspoiled and un-commercialised' a third of all people questioned agreed. Nearly three quarters found the island to be 'peaceful and relaxing'.

It was clear that the island attracted people who wanted a place that was relaxing, peaceful and unspoiled – unlike the south of England and London from where these visitors came. They also evidently bought into the 'Sunshine Island' slogan.

The questionnaire also probed the respondents on their activities the previous day. Two-thirds said they went for a walk, half did some shopping, a third sunbathed and a hardy 10% went swimming. This survey was the first of many over the next 50 years, showing how opinions changed or remained the same during the final burst of success for tourism – and its subsequent decline.

The 70s and 80s carried on the dramatic growth of visitors that had been seen in the 60s. The tourist survey of 1976, shows that most visitors still came from London and the south-east. Over half were first timers, as in the previous survey, so advertising and word of mouth was still working in favour of the island. Most came by air (53%), and 'peaceful atmosphere' was noted by 62% – which should have been a warning signal for the authorities as this had dropped from 75% in just five years. The same is true of another statement: asking respondents if Guernsey was 'an experience of a holiday abroad'. Fewer people responded positively to this statement, indicating that this positioning for the Guernsey brand had reached its sell-by date.

Another signal of potential storm clouds for the industry came in 1978. The President of the Guernsey Chamber of Commerce noted: 'We have experienced a season unlike others of recent years, whereby we were not fully booked in what has come to be accepted as the peak holiday months of the year'.[38] It seems that every time there was a clear sign that the tourist industry faced danger, the next year visitor numbers increased, as was the case in 1979. But equally, such positivity was immediately followed by another nail in the coffin. In 1980, BA ended all its routes to the island – replaced by local airlines, but was nevertheless the loss of a trusted carrier.

Back to the positives. In 1981, tourism became the number one contributor to the economy, representing 31% of income received from outside the island, ousting horticulture for the first time. This honour didn't last long though, as finance overtook it in 1983.[39] Visitor arrivals continued to grow until 1989, when tourist numbers reached an all-time high at around 450,000.

If the authorities in Guernsey adopted an ostrich approach to tourism and its competitors on the Continent throughout the 70s, the reality must have really hit home in 1979, when for the first time in history, the British spent more on holidays abroad than they did on holidays at home. Towards the end of the 70s, 2.5 million Britons went on package holidays and by 1986, that had risen to 10 million. The *coup de grâce* had arrived for the Guernsey tourist industry and sure enough in 1989, the peak was reached. Since that time, visitor numbers have been in free-fall.

The Decline Years

You'd think that writing about a sector of the economy that has only been around since 1815 would make life easy for the historian. That it would not be difficult to identify why the tourism industry has not continued to grow. After all, records are easily accessed, and many of the protagonists of the past 50 years or so, are still alive and can be spoken to face-to-face.

It turns out that tourism is an irritatingly tricky industry to cover. To put it simply, it has been a political football for the past 100 years and before that, back in the 19th century, a business treated apathetically by the Guernsey authorities. Every article, book and review on Guernsey tourism is therefore shot through with bias – either for or against growth or decline. And every statistic is a reminder of that old adage: 'There are lies, damn lies and statistics'.

Nevertheless, let's try to figure out why this important source of revenue lost its way after 1989. And our first culprit must be the sun. Guernsey rose to fame in the UK by being, together with Jersey, the sunniest part of the UK, with about 2,000 hours a year. As package holidays took off in the 60s and 70s, it became obvious to all potential tourists, that the Mediterranean offered more sunshine, with most resorts in Spain, Portugal and Italy delivering not only 40% more rays per year (2,800 hours), but also higher temperatures and less wind. If you wanted ideal beach weather, Guernsey didn't compete very well.

Next up as an explanation must come speed of getting to that sun. Since the early 70s, jets have transported passengers to the Mediterranean in around two hours – just an hour slower than flying to the island from Heathrow, and quicker by an hour than sailing from Poole. And travellers to Europe had any number of choices of airlines, destinations and starting airports. Guernsey airlines on the other hand, flew from a limited number of airports and used slower propeller-driven aircraft rather than jets.

And once you got to your destination, in the case of Europe, you could be taken to a new build, multi-story, modern hotel, complete with every mod-con you could desire. Guernsey on the other hand had not kept pace, and by-and-large, still offered fairly old-fashioned rooms and amenities.

Having dropped your bags at your hotel, in say Palma, the average Brit could stroll out from the hotel lobby, into pretty much guaranteed summer heat and sun, and dive into the warm waters of the hotel pool or sea. Or lie back on a waiting sunbed underneath a hotel umbrella or perhaps have paella in a local bistro. The whole resort, and the people servicing it, was built around pleasing you, the guest.

By comparison, in Guernsey the weather was less reliable, it can be wet in summer and the fog sirens do occasionally hoot. Your hotel may be near the beach, but the chances are that it was built back in the 30s. If you were in a guest house, it could be a bus ride from the coast. And staff were often not from Guernsey, as locals were either growing tomatoes, or increasingly, being lured to the finance industry with its modern offices, regular hours and high salaries. Hotels and guest houses relied on seasonal untrained workers, who had to be accommodated themselves, increasing the overheads of the business.

And in the evening, our British tourist in the Mediterranean could choose from the multitude of cafés, bars and restaurants along the beach front, or stay in their hotel and enjoy the entertainment. In Guernsey, the night-time offered plenty of choices, but ones that lacked the exoticism of a Spanish or Italian resort. St Peter Port provided fewer options than the visitor from London, Cardiff or Birmingham could find at home. Clearly the island suffered in comparison with its rivals and the authorities did little to compete effectively. In one of the Billets of 1987, there is a damning statement: '[There is] complacency both at political levels and in the industry regarding its situation and prospects'.[40] Not for the first time, Guernsey chose to shrug its shoulders and move on to the next big thing, rather than staying and fighting it out with its competitors.

Let's not forget though that despite no longer being the number one industry in the island after the early 80s, Guernsey continued to make good money from tourists. Let's look at the way that the island handled this industry at the end of the 20th century and into the 21st century.

Decline and Rebirth

Probably the best way to describe the past 30 years of tourism in the island is 'disinterested decline'. From the all-time high point of 1989, when 460,000 visitors came to the island, by 2019 that figure had declined by 40%. The biggest loss came in the last ten years of the 20th century, with each decade of the 21st century showing declines of 13% and 10% respectively.

So why do I call it a 'disinterested decline'? Some would say that it was a lack of political willingness to push this industry. In other words, the States did not feel inclined to invest heavily in advertising (a budget of £5.7 million in 1986) or support the industry in other ways.

But blaming the politicians is a bit too easy. You could argue they did not need to push the tourism sector too hard, as finance was booming. Not only was it the number one earner for the island (going from 11% of export earnings in 1973 to 51% in 1991), but it was also soaking up refugees from the fast-declining horticulture sector and welcoming an ever-diminishing number of school leavers with open arms. So, unlike tourism, which had to import its workers, finance employees were mostly local.

Such a relatively new sector for Guernsey did have to import experts, who had to live somewhere. And that gave an opportunity for guest house owners to shut down their ailing businesses and convert their properties into private homes for sale to finance gurus. We can see this in the decline of the guest house sector which had 39% of all beds in 1975, dropping to just 16% in 1983.[41] The politicians were also mindful of the fact that those tourists who came were not bringing in any more money in real terms in 1987 than they had done in 1975. Rex Birch, in a 1989 article put it as follows: 'A holidaymaker who stays in a hotel not Guernsey-owned, staffed by largely non-Guernsey people, eating food not grown on the island, driving cars hired from a non-Guernsey company and buying items in the shops which were brought in from outside the island. What is there in this for Guernsey?'[42]

Perhaps less emotionally, Peat Marwick who were commissioned by the States to carry out an economic appraisal of the island's economy felt that the small size of the island and its limited workforce were key factors. As they said in their 1987 report: '[Guernsey] is currently (and has historically been) dominated by one sector because the small size of the economy constrains the sustainable degree of diversification'.[43] In other words, there just aren't, and have never been, enough workers on the island to support the needs of more than one big business area. You can see this in the unemployment figures. In 1987 there were fewer than 1% of the workforce unemployed, which meant it was a sellers' market, driving up salaries and creating a level of inflation that had a negative effect on the competitiveness of the Guernsey tourist industry compared to its rivals. The Guernsey economy, according to Peat Marwick again, had grown in the 1980s at twice the rate of the British economy – no doubt reflecting the power of the new finance sector in the island.

This rise in the popularity of the finance sector for Guernsey workers had several spin-off consequences for the tourist industry. First of all, the higher salaries in finance meant that working in the hospitality industry was less attractive with its longer hours, often poor working conditions and the necessity to have a smile on your face 24x7. The Guernsey tourist business got less professional, less motivated and, as a consequence, visitor approval levels dropped – as noted by the Guernsey Chamber of Commerce in July 1989: 'The tourist board have had more complaints than usual this year about the quality of service from some of our commercial establishments'.[44]

Next, all those people earning good money in finance, driving from the outlying parishes into the St Peter Port finance hub, led to a busy-ness on roads not seen in previous generations. Wasn't this a good thing? Didn't it show how buoyant the Guernsey economy was at the end of the 20th century?

Let's go back briefly to the visitor surveys conducted by the local tourist board. In the very first such survey in 1975, the questionnaire asked visitors if they agreed that Guernsey was 'peaceful, quiet, relaxing and restful'. 62% or nearly two thirds said yes to this phrase.[45] Asking the same question in 1983, the positive response rate had dropped to 50%.[46] A really significant fall in such a short period of time.

What could have caused such a big drop? One answer, that is even truer today, concerns traffic. If anyone has driven from the airport to St Peter Port at rush hour, or tried to drive home from Town to St Sampson's after work, you'll know it can be a grindingly slow activity. Back in 1964, Guernsey had 15,000 cars pottering around the 400 miles of road on the island.[47] By 2018, that number had grown nearly six-fold to just over 84,000 vehicles (cars, motor bikes and commercial vehicles) for a population of around 62,000.[48] That's approximately 1,300 vehicles per thousand people. Wikipedia has a league table of motor vehicle density and at the top is tiny Gibraltar with a vehicle density of 1,444 cars per thousand people (expressed as 1,444/000), followed in second place by Guernsey. The EU has an average of 650/000 and the UK 600/000.[49] So, Guernsey smashes pretty much everybody with their vehicle density. Even Jersey has a much lower figure – 674/000.

If you wanted 'peace, quiet, relaxation and rest', I doubt you'd be happy dodging cars, inhaling fumes and generally feeling uptight with the frenetic activity going on around you on the roads. Hardly the place to have a quiet stroll or peaceful peddle. And this was clearly seen to be a particular issue already back in 1978, when the annual visitor survey revealed, according to the *Guernsey Press* at the time:

> A survey showed that visitors thought that traffic was a serious problem and most felt something needed to be done to ease congestion in Town.

Back in the 50s and 60s, Guernsey was a mecca for young families looking for sea and ice creams, bucket and spade holidays. By the 80s and 90s those families had seen their kids leave home, and parents were now maybe occupying more senior, stressful jobs. They had the memories of fun times on the beaches of the island (more than half were returning vacationers) and now, they wanted

6: BUCKETS, SPADES & WINDBREAKS

a peaceful relaxing holiday. Not what you get with an island buzzing with cars.

This last point is important in trying to understand the dive in visitor numbers after 1989. Our arrivals cohort after the 70s was increasingly an older, affluent age group from the south of England, without kids, arriving by air and knowing the island from previous visits – in 1991, 56% of arrivals had been to the island before. They wanted good food, good service, comfortable accommodation, relaxing daytimes and entertaining evenings. Their demands were unfortunately not met in full. The States noted in the Billet of 1991: 'The concern must be that there is a comparative lack of investment in hostelries and a consequent move downmarket as facilities deteriorate'.[50]

As we entered the 21st century, another issue arose. Guernsey was haemorrhaging visitors in the peak summer months to the Mediterranean resorts, but potential visitors could still be attracted to the idea of a short spring or autumn break in the island. Unfortunately, this concept of the long weekend brought in new competitors for Guernsey. Now short visits to cultural capitals came into play – both in the UK as well as in Europe: Paris, Prague, Bath, and York became new rivals for visitors.

We can see this new trend towards different types of holidays play out in the number of days visitors spent on the island, and it was recognised by the States in a Billet of 1991: 'Many (visitors) now regard Guernsey as a second holiday or short break tourist resort'.[51] This wind of change clearly disturbed the States, particularly the Treasury, as was noted in the Guernsey Chamber of Commerce *Contact* magazine in 1993: 'The States resolved that the development of the island's visitor economy was of strategic importance and that policies should be adopted which saw a return in the number of visitor arrivals to a level which was achieved in 1989'.[52] (ie 450,000)

Not for the first time in Guernsey's history, the politicians had suddenly woken up to the fact that their second biggest money earner was declining fast. Their panic was hardly a surprise, given that in 1989, tourism brought in well over £100 million to the States. In 1973, horticulture and tourism together represented 66% of the export economy, in 1991 that had shrunk to just 23%.[53]

The 1992 budget for the Tourist Board was increased by over 7% to £3 million (2% of the States total budget), a target set to increase bed numbers back to 12,000 from the 10,000 at the end of the 80s. And a change of heart by creating both long and short-term licenses for imported seasonal workers. Overall, the politicians targeted the Tourist Board with an increase of 5% in visitor numbers.

This change of heart was spurred on by the big drop in visitor numbers in 1991, reflecting the so-called Lawson recession caused by high-interest rates, falling house prices and an overvalued exchange rate. To borrow an expression, every time the UK sneezed, Guernsey caught a cold. And in 1991, over three million people were out of work on the mainland, many of whom may well have considered a holiday on the island. These people also faced huge mortgage repayments which dampened demand for holidays.

The politicians had woken up. As the Chamber of Commerce put it in 1994: 'The States has declared its support for the industry, tourism is no longer a dirty word'.[54] More money was released to get holidaymakers to the island and now it was up to the Tourist Board to spend this money wisely. They needed a strategy.

Reading the 1990s editions of the Guernsey Chamber of Commerce *Contact* magazine, the issue of coherent strategy came up time and time again. Get the bed numbers up. No, sell the bed numbers you've got. Be broad in appeal. No, go for the upmarket traveller. Focus on the summer. No, concentrate on the shoulder months. Spend more money on advertising. No, most of it is wasted. And a particular bugbear — attract more visitors from the Continent. No, it's money wasted as our real market is the UK. A good example of this debate over strategy can be seen in this quotation from Stuart Falla, head of the construction company RG Falla: 'Tourism ... should not be encouraged to spend money changing "the product". People should accept the island for what it is; we are not and never will be a cheap resort'.[55]

One way or another, politicians and hoteliers got up real heads of steam over the tourist strategy. And over the amount it contributed to the exchequer. The reality was that the halcyon days of the 60s, 70s and 80s would never return. The world market for holidays had become huge (some say it is now the world's largest industry) and the options enormous. From a marketing point of view, the only solution was to become a successful niche destination.

Oh dear! That strategy may have been the underlying intention but, for it to work, as John Gollop noted in the Chamber of Commerce *Contact* magazine in 1996: 'All sections of our tourist industry must be confident that the island's strategy fully represents their interests. This is clearly not the case'.[56]

The transport side of the Guernsey holiday 'product' — getting people quickly, cheaply and conveniently to the island, certainly were not convinced that visitor numbers would grow. Air UK sold its Guernsey slots at Heathrow in 1998, KLM withdrew flights from the island in 1999 and Condor was given a monopoly of sea transport to the Bailiwick in 1998 — despite a recognised poor level of service. Rodney Brouard put this issue of transport succinctly in 2000: 'Tourism will continue to decline as bed numbers reduce. Fewer tourists will mean fewer aircraft and ferry seats being filled; services to Guernsey will be reduced'.[57]

Hoteliers and restaurant owners were also not fully on board with the Tourist Board's strategy of targeting potential visitors from the Continent as well as the UK. Advertising to the latter increased. In 1995, the Board spent £700,000 on media on the Continent, rising to £1.3 million in 1998 (a level just under the amount spent for the UK). Many regarded this as a gross over-investment as 'only one third of visitors come from Europe'.[58] Investment to attract Continental visitors was stopped in 2003, mainly because routes from mainland Europe to Guernsey were so poor. In 2019, that figure of one third remains true, with UK visitors now representing 67% of arrivals compared to 98% in 1970 – so you could say that in the long term the Board had done the right thing with its targeting.

Looking back on the first decade of the 21st century, one can see a lack of agreement on what to do about tourism. Someone needed to step up, take ownership of the problem and lead the industry forward. There was no one to do that and dithering and delay continued, with clear consequences. The number of beds available continued to drop, falling to just 5,000 in 2017 – fewer than just after World War 2, and three times fewer than in the heyday of 1967. Many small hotels and bed & breakfast establishments disappeared. Even worse, despite the drop in bed numbers, the Chamber of Commerce in 2008 noted that occupancy rates were down to just 50% – when break-even required a rate of 65%, and when London hotels were achieving 90%.[59] Finally on the subject of accommodation, in 2003 Carl Symes of the Guernsey Hotel and Tourist Association (GHATA) made the statement that: 'It costs 50% more to build a hotel room in Guernsey than it does in England'.[60] Finishing this pretty negative review at the start of the new Millennium, there is an interesting interview with Tom Castledine in the *Contact* magazine of December 2002. Tom clearly hadn't had a very good Christmas, as you can read: 'I can see nothing on the horizon that will improve tourism in Guernsey. When the island lost the powerboat racing and the Swan Regatta

– those were signs that things would never be the same again'.[61] And poor Tom didn't know then about the global banking crash of 2008 that did nothing for the tourist industry on the island.

A Brighter Future?

Is there a positive end to this story about the tourist industry? Looking at the visitor numbers for the present day, the answer should be no – numbers are still dropping. But here comes a different way of looking at things. Head count doesn't mean everything. 'Paid Leisure' – as Stuart Pinnell of Visit Guernsey called the old definition of tourism – is no longer an adequate description of today's travellers to the Bailiwick.

The industry needs to look at itself through fresh eyes. Just as in consumer product markets, some brands rely on big volumes and low prices, but there are others that look more at their profitability per item sold, and are quite happy with low numbers but high profits.

This is part of the answer for tourism and where it stands today. After many years of debate, it looks like the politicians and hospitality workers have finally agreed that Guernsey is a long weekend/short break destination. More than that, it is the place for older, cash- and time-rich people who want: 'nothing more than a few days break to potter. Not long haul but miles away'.[62]

Instead of trying to copy Mallorca, two-week package holidays and family fun for young and old, the local leaders finally woke up and realised that this was a ridiculous dream for a little island. The future became about profitably servicing visitors on short, refreshing breaks within the infrastructure of high quality, highly serviced 5,000 beds/bedrooms.

And not just any visitors. The Tourist Board in 2002 woke up to the reality that the island had become a short stay destination.

They also realised it was somewhere for special interest seekers to come. As Geoff Norman, President of the Tourist Board, noted in 2002: 'We appreciate that there is no use in having a scattergun approach to tourism. The industry needs to be focused and able to offer attractions to special interest visitors like bird watchers and those wanting to learn about Guernsey's history'.[63]

Another change of attitude was a realisation that tourism and the finance industry could be positive partners rather than competitors. It turns out that there is a synergy between the two that is of benefit for both. The booming finance sector generated lots of well-paid locals, who wanted to spend some of their money on restaurants and entertaining their friends or their clients. They needed top quality eating establishments. And guess what – so did our well-healed mini-break visitors. Today very good restaurants can be found all over the island.

Older couples over from London and the south-east for a long weekend wanted to be pampered in well-equipped comfortable hotels. And that was exactly what business travellers to the island also wanted. Today, high quality large and small hotels are dotted across the island. They would not look out of place in any large city around the world.

And for a small island of just 60,000 people, the communications links are infinitely better than any equivalent sized town in the UK (think equivalent-sized Castleford, Hereford, Margate or Stroud). In 2019, the airport operated ten routes across the UK and Jersey. Of course, some of the old Guernsey attitudes remain. The airport runway was extended in 2014, but still remains too short for Airbus 320s or Boeing 737s.

Sea transport is also alive with two ferry companies operating six routes to the island. Again, Guernsey still doesn't get it quite right. The main ferry company Condor, operates its *Liberation* high-speed trimaran from Poole to the Channel Islands, transporting a maximum of 800 passengers. It looks great, cost £50 million, but unfortunately has regular problems, which continue to irritate passengers over four years into service.

> Condor's lack of communication and regular sailing problems have put some visitors off returning to the island.[64]

In the second decade of the 21st century, tourism contributes significantly to the island economy. The BBC reported in March 2020 that visitors spent £146 million in 2019, with an average spend per head of £704.[65] The island now has decent hotels, both large and small, it has excellent restaurants and a unspoilt coastline. It is just 45 minutes from Gatwick, still less from Southampton and only three hours by sea from Poole. It offers easy visits to the other islands, a living museum of a landscape, with relics from many thousands of years of occupancy and a variety of outdoor pursuits for the athletic and the less lithe. Despite all this, a report by PwC in 2017 on tourism says that the island is perceived by potential visitors as expensive to get to, with limited things to do when they get there. The report suggests that the States' ambition to attract 3% more visitors each year looks difficult to achieve.[66]

Will tourism go the way of knitting, privateering, quarrying and horticulture – leaving memories and traces but nothing more? The graph of visitor numbers doesn't look encouraging, but the synergy with finance is valuable, and the long-term boom in tourism worldwide should encourage the authorities to invest in the industry. It is up against massive competition and needs to maintain a level of awareness in the UK and the Continent. More than that, the States have recognised (and pledged money) that they need to do more to open new departure destinations in both the UK and on the Continent. Above all, the island needs to clearly stand for something – a unique selling proposition (USP) that stays strong in potential visitor's minds.

And to end this chapter, let's look at a new area of tourism that has boomed in recent years – cruise ships.

Cruise Ships

The start of this chapter discussed the geographical benefits of the island and how it spurred the development of tourism. In the 21st century, geography again waved its magic wand in the Bailiwicks direction, as anyone driving down the Val des Terres and turning onto the South Esplanade will testify, as they might well be confronted with the sight of a behemoth of a cruise ship moored in the Little Russel.

The cruise ship business worldwide has had a relatively short modern history. Some say it all started with the daft American series *The Love Boat* in the 70s. More serious-minded analysts would say it was the arrival of middle-age for the baby boomers that sparked this new type of 'holiday as adventure'.

This cohort had grown up as adventurous tourists, visiting far-flung places as hippies, enjoying golfing holidays around the world in early middle age, popularising skiing and surfing. But, as the legs got stiffer, so some of the get-up-and-go in baby boomers began to evaporate. They still wanted adventure, still wanted to visit new destinations but now wanted comfortable beds, nice food and no hassle.

Cruising was the perfect answer. A floating posh hotel with plenty of amenities that did all the hard work of getting you to interesting cities and resorts. Plus, as the ships got bigger and bigger, the value for money improved – Royal Caribbean's *Oasis of the Sea* launched in 2009 catered for 6,000 passengers with 2,000 crew.

6: BUCKETS, SPADES & WINDBREAKS

Cruise liners offered all sorts of destinations and amongst them were two that opened a door for Guernsey. Many northern Europeans are desperate for the sun at the end of their dismal winters and the Mediterranean is where they want to be. So why not jump on a ship near your home in Sweden, Britain, Germany or Holland and be gently whisked to the warmth of Spain, or Italy, on a floating luxury hotel? Or maybe you just want to discover a bit more of the UK by being able to circumnavigate it.

Of course, en route, passengers don't want to be just staring at the sea 24x7. They want interesting distractions, and this is where Guernsey's geography is perfect. Halfway between northern Europe and the Mediterranean, it's an ideal stopping-off point. The same is true for round Britain voyages – the island is a good starting or end point.

Its longitude and latitude weren't the only benefits. The Little Russel between Guernsey and Herm, provides good shelter, adequate water depth and good holding, close to the harbour of St Peter Port – aspects their rival Jersey can't offer.

Guernsey was added to the cruise ships' itineraries at the end of the 90s and, by 2008, 45 ships stopped at the island, 60 in 2010 and 117 in 2017.[67] This dropped a little in 2018 and 2019, partly reflecting bad weather which caused some liners not to stop. Each time one of these monsters dropped anchor, tenders would ferry up to 3,000 people ashore, where they would shop, drop into a café or pub, take a coach trip around the island or stroll around town. Most would spend up to four hours ashore and although they don't spend a lot of money individually (average was £36 in 2017), with so many coming on to the island, it added up in 2017 to £4 million in revenue for Guernsey from 110,000 liner passengers.

Perhaps of potential greater value to Guernsey than visitor spending is the fact that more than 100,000 cruise ship passengers a year are exposed for a few hours to the charm of the Bailiwick. Potentially a far more effective form of advertising than press or TV. Research suggests that about 3% of overnight-stay visitors originally came to the island on a cruise ship. So this new aspect of tourism could really be seen as awareness advertising more than just revenue earning.

It seems the local authorities have grasped this amazing free awareness benefit, as can be seen on days when a cruise ship arrives. Throughout St Peter Port, the narrow shopping streets often echo to the sounds of local musicians playing for visitors. A truly carnival atmosphere is created.

Of course, Guernsey being Guernsey and not wanting to overdo the welcome spirit (unlike other cruise ship destinations, eg Orkney); there are no pier facilities and so passengers must be ferried ashore by tender boats, which can be quite an experience in choppy seas. Nevertheless, the island has been voted the number one cruise ship destination in the UK by industry experts.

After 200 years, the tourism industry remains a key component of the island economy. It has moved from a dilettante destination for Victorian gentlemen, to the bucket and spade holiday of the 60s and 70s. Today it is a long weekend break or cruise liner stop-off, with a support infrastructure of large modern hotels and boutique establishments. And it benefits from a synergistic relationship with the finance community, resulting in a high number of good restaurants at both ends of the price spectrum.

Guernsey as tourist destination is our sixth Guernsey 'brand' and has been the first to live happily alongside another Guernsey service. Now it's time to turn to the story of our seventh reinvention, the offshore finance industry.

7: Offshore or Offside?

Our chapter on tourism covered an industry that is positively cuddly compared to the current dominant business of the island, and subject of the last chapter in this book, financial services.

I am not a financial expert. This meant I approached writing about Guernsey's latest 'brand' with considerable trepidation. But I also began it with a mission – to explain this business in everyday language and not to get seduced by complicated explanations from experts.

The story of the growth of financial services has echoes of earlier chapters but also has some aspects we have not seen in any of the previous big money-earners for the island.

Perhaps its closest relative in Guernsey history is privateering. Just like the slightly dubious activities of 18th century ships' crews, financial services use legislative loopholes to make a living. Just like privateers, it attracts a lot of support businesses. Just like privateers, it is disliked intensely by rivals. And just like privateers, it makes some people very rich.

Perhaps the most difficult part of writing this chapter is working out what's true and what is, to put it politely, hot air. Mark Hampton describes the difficulty in his excellent and dispassionate appraisal of offshore finance centres: 'The mechanisms of how offshore finance actually operates are often hidden behind the somewhat impenetrable jargon of international business and tax laws'.[1] This is putting it mildly. It's a jungle of intertwined finance businesses, government interventions and counter interventions and, in the eye of the storm, our tiny island. And let's face it, as in our previous chapters, we have seen how the island has often found itself in this position.

It is however unlike any previous economic activities on the island in that financial services is essentially an intellectual business – it doesn't use the physical attributes on the island. It doesn't have a tangible product. It is the island's first digital economic activity and a very 21st century enterprise. The one thing this industry does have in common with all the previous business activities of the island was well put by the authors of the 1967 Outline Development Plan for the island. In it they say the following: '[We] import money by the sale of the produce of the soil (Tomatoes). [We] import money by the sale of enjoyment (Tourism). The important thing is that we import money'.[2] This prescient statement in the Billet was somewhat spoilt by another remark by the Deputies at the time who noted: 'Land is the platform of all human activity'. How wrong were they to be?

Before we tell the story of financial services though, we should take a sidestep and introduce the business that acted as the pathfinder for Guernsey's move into the modern digital world. And, for once in this book, we can readily pinpoint when, and by whom, a new local industry was created.

Tektronix

In 1958, Guernsey was essentially a tomato island. The late 50s saw its export of the fruit reach a plateau that was exceeded only once in the rest of the 20th century. It employed 25% of the population, with tourism the next most important – two industries based on sunlight and the warmth of its latitude.

The island's economy in the late 50s was what you might call cosy. Shielded by UK legislation, its tomatoes enjoyed special privileges on the mainland. Its tourist industry, likewise protected by foreign exchange restrictions, made the island the nearest thing a UK resident could get to a foreign holiday. Both industries were established and had been so for several generations. Things just sort of rolled along in a predictable way.

This all changed in 1958, with the arrival of a scouting party – from the future. A young, balding ex-US Air Force pilot, Al Hannmann, came to Guernsey on holiday to visit his English wife's brother and, possibly more importantly for him, to buy a tax-free Austin Healey. Apparently, Al had lusted after this classic British open-topped sports car for years, and had asked his brother-in-law to let him know if one came up for sale on the island.

Al worked in Europe for a fast-growing American west coast electronics company called Tektronix. They made test and control equipment called oscilloscopes, which measured electric impulses and showed them on a little screen. Although based in a small Zurich office, Al was on a mission to find somewhere in Europe for the American company to set up a manufacturing base, for supplying customers of their booming European business, promptly and cost efficiently.

This mission became a topic of casual conversation during a drinks party with neighbours at his brother-in-law's house. Hearing about Al's project, one of the guests told him that there was a big empty factory just down the road and, if he had time during his holiday, he should have a look. Al was a man of action and visited the site in Victoria Avenue, about halfway between St Peter Port and St Sampson's. The disused factory turned out to be an empty weaving mill, in the shelter of a disused quarry, and was originally owned by a textiles company called Fabrique Industrielle which had shut down its operations in the island some years earlier.

Al's serendipitous 'nose' around an empty shell of a building, amazingly, led to the organisation setting up a manufacturing operation on the island. Al suggested this location to the owners of Tektronix by sending them a telegram: he'd found the perfect place for their European factory, but only gave them its longitude and latitude![3]

Although the directors of the company were initially sceptical of the idea of a tiny speck in the English Channel as a future European home, the logic for Guernsey became highly attractive. The islanders spoke English (important for the four non-linguist Tektronix owners), goods from Guernsey could enter the UK duty free and the EU ('Common Market' at the time) also respected the island's duty-free status; transport links were good for both the Continent and England; and finally, the island had plenty of well-educated labour. An added bonus was the helpful attitude of the States of Guernsey, who saw in Tektronix a new source of tax revenue, a step into the future, and finally a business not defined by sunshine or soil.

In an article in the *The Star* on 1 September 1958, the debate by the Royal Court on the value of allowing this foreign company to set up on the island was reported. The newspaper remarked on the States' pragmatic discussions of the benefits of leasing out the disused weaving mill in Victoria Avenue as follows: 'The building was a large one. The premises had been idle and were not likely to be in ready demand by a local enterprise'. So in 1958, the States granted Tektronix an initial two-year lease with the option of buying the Victoria Avenue site for £40,000. And thus began Guernsey's first tentative steps into the modern world of business.

The Tektronix story lasted 32 years (leaving the island in 1990), eventually covering two factories (Victoria Avenue plus a huge custom-built site near the airport), employing as many as 600 people in the 1980s, and becoming Guernsey's largest single employer. On which Frank Doyle, an early employee of the local company, noted: 'When Tek first started recruiting in Guernsey, we literally employed everyone on the island who knew what Ohm's law was'.[4]

As well as opening local people's eyes to a new electronic world, Tektronix more importantly brought modern American business practices to the island. Simple things, like using first names for all employees, providing a company-wide profit-sharing scheme, everyone eating in the same canteen, annual picnics on Herm and educating employees about the workings of electronic devices. Tektronix was in many respects the bridge between the old world of horticulture and tourism to a new digital world.

In an article by the Guernsey Chamber of Commerce, mourning the departure of the company, they noted: 'During its 30 years here, the company has set standards in training, staff relationships and salary scales which have had to be emulated by others'.[5] These modern business practices that Tektronix introduced, and which were enthusiastically taken up by their employees, acted as a sort of fertiliser on the Guernsey population. They showed the islanders that employment did not have to mean becoming either an agricultural worker or a hospitality provider in the tourist industry. There was an alternative. One that didn't require grubby hands or a permanent smile.

Another Fertilizer

If Tektronix showed the island that tomatoes and sandcastles were not the only ways to make a living, then there was another key ingredient that made the financial services industry possible.

The 50s and 60s were decades of austerity in the UK. Tax rates were eye-wateringly high for entrepreneurs (up to 98%), unemployment rose steadily from a low of 1% in the mid-50s to a high of 14% in 1983, foreign exchange restrictions were in place and sterling was devalued 14% by the Wilson government in 1967. Adding further misery was an upward growth of inflation, from a low of under 1% at the end of the 50s to ten times that by 1971.

You can imagine how people with some wealth in the UK found themselves living in a fiscal nightmare. But someone can always make money out of people's misery and, in this case, it was Guernsey. The States saw the opportunity to offer the wealthy in the UK a way out of their pain. They introduced a new housing policy: a two-tier system which enabled the wealthy to move to this low taxation island by buying 'open market' houses – attracting inward migration without impacting the cost of property for the locals who bought houses classed as 'local market'. This two-tier housing system was just part of a concerted effort to attract *rentiers* to the island, who would not only boost tax-income for the States but also inject fresh entrepreneurial blood into the population. The housing system was further augmented by the introduction of special local market housing for essential workers – people with specialist skills not available amongst the local population. This was no doubt triggered by Tektronix's need for experts to help expand their operations.

A key element to attract incomers was taxation. The Bailiwick had long had low taxes to help maintain its benefits to the local population and minimise emigration but, in 1960, the States reduced still further the level of income tax from 26% down to 20% (where it remains today). *Rentiers* did indeed find the island appealing, particularly after the building of an estate of large, detached properties in the old military stronghold of Fort George. In a 1975 interview, one of the builders of the Fort George estate expressed his reasons for settling on the island as follows:

> Well, the wife and I decided many years ago, that we'd settle in the Channels Islands when we retired and when we started this development on Fort George, we liked the people and the island, and we decided to settle here. We were concerned that sooner or later one of the governments might do as they've

done and that was to tax very heavily unearned income. I have no pension as such so that any taxation on unearned income is in fact what would otherwise be my pension.[6]

By 1991 there were around 800 of these *rentiers* who were living at that time on declared investment incomes of £25,000 or more and represented in that year approximately 20% of Guernsey's GDP. They too had need of financial services and still represent a significant proportion of tax paid in the island today.

To sum it all up – the combination of a static horticulture industry and a 'not as sunny as Spain' ailing tourist business, plus the blueprint of Tektronix and the purposeful legislation of the States – all meant that by the early 60s, the island was ripe for a new white-collar industry.

Financial Services – The Early Days

Up until now, we have not really needed to define the product or service behind each new business revolution on the island. Knitting is clear, as is smuggling, shipbuilding, quarrying, tomato growing and tourism. But this new business on the island, 'offshore financial services', what on earth does that mean?

My best and shortest definition would be: 'Offshore financial services exist to help people pay less tax'.

Dress it up in fancy language if you will but it really does come down to paying less tax. And to help people or companies do that, the local financial services industry has many organisations to guide, manage and action money management for clients. These include: banks, insurance companies, investment managers, stockbrokers, trustees, mutual fund administrators, accountancy firms, plus support services like IT, legal and accountancy firms. Unlike the origins of Tektronix in Guernsey, the birth of the island's financial services industry has no obvious founding father. Instead, there are two possible theories about how this dominant employer of locals in the 21st century came into existence. We'll take each in turn and try to explain them dispassionately.

Origins of Financial Services: The 'Self-Interest' Theory

The first possible way that Guernsey's financial services started can be termed the 'self-interest' theory. And it is a familiar story in this book, reflecting a series of decisions taken elsewhere which had consequences for individuals around the world, as well as for the island. To learn more about this version of how the local financial services started, I came across an early 1970s Open University TV course called *Making Sense of Society*.[7] One of the programmes had an interview in 1974, with Stewart Faulkner, the Guernsey manager of a recently arrived merchant bank. His version of the beginnings of the local banking sector provides some interesting clues.

In his interview, Faulkner explained that in the 50s and early 60s, Great Britain had an organisation in Africa which managed certain common functions like the postal network, telecommunications and the collection of some taxes for Uganda, Kenya and Tanganyika. This organisation was called the East African Commission.

In 1961, the process of decolonisation was underway, and as part of it, the Commission planned to introduce the obligation for residents to register for the imposition of estate duties. In other words, on death, locals were going to have their estates taxed. To avoid this, they needed to get their wealth out of the East African colonies and into more friendly jurisdictions. Their money was in sterling and so Guernsey was one of the obvious places for their capital, as the island imposed no death duties. And to manage the resultant in-flow of money, merchant banks started to appear on the island.

In his interview for the Open University in the early 1970s, Mr Faulkner also identified something else, putting it rather bluntly: 'Going back ten to fifteen years, one had in the islands quite large sums of money deposited here by people working overseas in the Commonwealth and the Dominions who avoided admitting it to the United Kingdom for tax considerations'.[8] Guernsey paid interest on money deposited in local banks gross – so no income tax was imposed.

Faulkner goes on to say that the second trigger for the flight of capital by individuals to the island was the introduction in 1965/66 of the capital gains tax in the UK. Capital gains are the positive difference between the sale price of an asset and its original purchase price – if you like, the difference between what you paid for your first house and what you sold it for. It was introduced by the then chancellor Jim Callaghan to stop people avoiding income tax through switching their money from income into capital.

To bypass this new capital gains tax, people would transfer the ownership of their assets into a trust. We'll talk about trusts in more detail later but briefly, a trust is an arrangement where the owner of assets hands them over to a trust, who manage them for the benefit of a person or people identified by the original owner. Initially these trusts were set up in the UK, but the profits from the investment management of the trust funds, whilst exempt from capital gains tax, would still be liable for income tax. So, at some point, a smart UK accountant may well have said to his or her client, you know you could reduce your income tax by moving the trust fund to Guernsey where only local income tax is levied – at 20%. They may also have whispered that trusts in Guernsey were (at that time) secret and the owner's name was not revealed. This establishment of trusts on the island was accelerated in 1969, by the further tightening up of Capital Gains and Estate Duty rules, which led to many more UK trusts moving to Guernsey.

Faulkner also talked about another push factor towards more investment in Guernsey. One of the conditions for the UK admission into the then European Common Market, was to reduce the so-called sterling area – the group of countries that either linked their currencies to the pound, or used pounds for their currency. Within this area, capital could be moved freely with no exchange controls.

The result of the reduction of the sterling area was that some banks in the Caribbean, finding themselves suddenly outside the sterling area, moved some of their operations to Guernsey. A good example is the Royal Bank of Canada, which moved to the island in the early 70s and whose local manager in an interview outlined their relocation reasons as follows: 'a place to look after our Caribbean business which had to come back to the sterling area'.[9]

This 'self-interest' origins story can be clearly seen in the growth in the number of merchant banks settling in Guernsey to manage the affairs of both individuals and companies who had moved their money to the island. The first bank, Kleinwort Benson, arrived in 1963 and, thanks to the various pieces of UK legislation during the 60s, by 1974 there were 43 banks on the island.

Outside activities may well have triggered this financial services boom because, as we have already seen, local Guernsey laws topped up the flow of money into the island with the arrival of the *rentiers*, who were defined by the States in a Billet of 1992 as: 'those persons who live primarily on investment income, generally derived from activities outside the island'.[10] They too had need of financial services and still represent a significant proportion of tax paid in the island today.

This 'self-interest' story has a nice, serendipitous quality. It probably would be approved by the financial services industry itself, as it seems quite innocuous. It reflects a simple insight: people with assets want to protect them from government tax legislation, and so are looking for ways to both shield and grow these assets. To put some statistics behind this sense of grievance against UK government tax legislation, here is a quotation from John Langlois who was speaking at an Institute of Directors' conference in the late 90s: '(In the early days) tax rates in some countries were horrendous. A top rate in the UK of 83% on earned income, 98% on unearned income and marginal rates of 102%'.[11] So financial services in Guernsey exist because of this consumer need to avoid wealth being attacked by governments. But that's just one version of the possible origins of today's dominant business. There is another, rather murkier version.

Origins of Financial Services: The 'Top-Down' Theory

Our first theory on why Guernsey has become an offshore financial centre is a sort of bottom-up explanation – individuals around the world trying to protect their wealth from what they consider to be over-zealous tax authorities. Our second version starts from the other end – and is a top-down explanation.

Explanation is perhaps an exaggeration, as this theory is shrouded in mystery and I am not sure anyone has, or is prepared to give, a clear answer. The story starts after World War 2 and has two main, but intertwined, strands: the decline of the British Empire and the growth of power by Russia and the USA.

Let's start with the decline of the British Empire. Decolonisation had been happening for some time in the 20th century and reached a key turning point in 1956, with what is called the Suez crisis. The Suez Canal, although built by the French, had become part-owned by the British when Egypt's share was bought by Disraeli, who saw the need to protect this vital short cut from the East to Great Britain.

In the 50s, nationalism in Egypt had grown with animosity towards the British who maintained troops in the country, despite ostensibly giving Egypt independence back in the 1930s. Things came to a head in 1956, when Britain refused to finance the building of the Aswan dam on the Nile. Egypt's political head, President Nasser, retaliated by nationalising the canal, planning to use its revenue to pay for the dam.

This was unacceptable to both the British and French, who used a willing surrogate, Israel, to attack Egypt. They were joined by their two allies who took back the canal in several armed battles. The rest of the world reacted furiously to this rather old-fashioned colonial power-play and, in particular, the USA would not tolerate this situation. Britain and France were threatened with sanctions by the US President Eisenhower, plus vague, menacing suggestions of nuclear reprisals from Russia. Britain and France backed down and in effect this was the moment they gave up their status as world powers. The British Empire influence was never the same again.

But what's that got to do with Guernsey and financial services? Here we need to focus on the City of London, which was the banker for the British Empire. It gave out the money in loans needed for the investment in exploiting the agricultural, mineral and commodity wealth of the colonies. These riches of Empire came flowing back to Great Britain and more precisely into the deep coffers of the City's banks.

You can imagine how the cosy life of the bankers of the City of London had been shattered by Suez, and the realisation that the colonial game was up and there were new global bosses. What would become of the banks' profits in this new world order? Would the bankers shrug their shoulders and accept they had been relegated to bit players? The answer was a resounding no. The City of London fought back and replaced Britain's role as a colonial power by becoming the world's dominant financial centre. And this transformation started with a clever piece of jiggery-pokery called the Eurodollar market.

After World War 2, the pound sterling, which had been the world's most important currency for business transactions (founded on the old system of backing every bank note with an equivalent amount of gold), began losing out to the dollar. As the USA increased its manufacturing power, it imported more and more raw materials and paid for them in dollars. And that meant there were dollars sloshing around the world, not owned by US residents. At the same time, the Russians were also dollar-rich thanks to their dollar-denominated oil revenues.

Initially, these dollars were deposited in domestic banks outside the USA, who sent them back to American banks where they were invested in the US money markets. These markets then provided loans to American companies wanting to buy materials from foreign suppliers, who demanded payment in dollars. Unfortunately, various long-standing laws in the States made it hard for banks to grow and, as US corporations got bigger and more successful, the US banks found it increasingly difficult to service these clients.

Despite this constraint, the growth of the American economy led to a balance of payments deficit and so the US government started making foreign transactions in dollars more and more difficult, such as placing ceilings on interest due on US deposits held by foreigners. As you can imagine, owners of these dollars didn't appreciate this restriction, and sought a way of maintaining the use of this currency for their activities. And amongst these disgruntled dollar account holders were Russians, who were worried that, because of the Cold War, the Americans might freeze their assets.

What happened was inevitable. Foreign owners of US dollar accounts began moving their money out of America, and into mainly European banks, but still in dollars. This money became known as Eurodollars. And European banks used these deposits as loans to other customers of their bank. In particular, UK banks found Eurodollars were a good way around their government's 1957 banning of sterling for financing foreign trade between third parties. So initially the Eurodollar market was partly created by an unwitting push from the USA who were trying to protect their balance of payments. Now comes the pull bit or the jiggery-pokery mentioned earlier. And guess what? It appears we can identify the source of this sleight-of-hand.

The Midland Bank had become the largest deposit bank in the world by 1919, and was the first British bank to set up a foreign exchange department. It had a real international outlook and was the London bank for over 600 correspondent banks around the world. In 1955, the Midland began deliberately acquiring US dollars by offering a higher rate of interest on 30-day deposits than the maximum allowed in the USA. The Midland then sold these dollars and bought sterling at an exchange rate lower than the Bank of England. This attracted a lot of interest from dollar holders, and in one month (June 1955), the Midland saw $49 million coming into the bank. In technical terms this buying and simultaneous selling is called arbitrage.

The Midland had invented a new product. One based first on the insight that US dollar holders were unable to lend all the money they wanted, due to US government restrictions, and therefore needed an alternative home which was less restrictive. A second insight was simply that as nobody before had thought about this profitable use of arbitrage, the chances were that it would probably be allowed by the authorities. And thirdly, the Midland knew they had potential clients for loans. In the UK entrepreneurs were crying out for money but were restricted in borrowings, as part of government anti-inflation policy.

This Midland bank story has been very well documented by Professor Catherine Schenk, in a 1999 article on the origins of the London Eurodollar market. In it, she quotes from a Bank of England correspondence: 'The Bank of England was concerned that Midland probably should have sought exchange control, that the interest offered was too high and that the subsequent swaps violated the spirit of monetary constraint pursued by the Government'.[12]

But even if there was some hesitation, the Bank of England did not try to stop the Midland with this new activity. The bank's creativity was soon picked up by competitors in the City, particularly the merchant banks, as opposed to the clearing banks. And as the Eurodollar market grew, the Bank of England and the UK Treasury continued to quietly allow the loophole to remain. As Professor Schenk notes: 'There was a consensus that London should remain an important financial centre and that restricting the new business through invasive action was inadvisable'.[13]

Lucky London, and its banks, were also helped by the polar opposite attitude of other European banks, who worried about this new 'hot money' (Professor Schenk's term) and generally refused to offer credit interest on these foreign deposits. This negative attitude by European banks was reinforced by President Kennedy who introduced an 'Interest Equalization tax' to stop Americans getting preferential interest in the European market. This actually had the effect of US corporations moving their capital out of the States, into European banks. All this really boosted the London business and was underwritten by the Bank of England who noted in 1963: 'However much we dislike hot money we cannot be international bankers and refuse to accept money. We cannot have an international currency and deny its use internationally'.[14]

'Hot Money'? If you are an entrepreneur anywhere in the world and you want to be paid for a service or commodity, you want the money you get to be safe – one that everyone accepts, one that won't lose its value overnight. And from the 1950s onwards, that safe currency was the US dollar, backed by its equivalent of gold in Fort Knox.

Paying a wheat grower or an oil producer in dollars is hardly 'hot', but those dollars also could be used to buy or sell drugs, to pay or receive bribes, in fact to oil the criminal black market in all its forms. And in the early days, the London banks accepted any dollars without too much checking or interference from the Bank of England. In the film *The Spider's Web* (2017), Professor Ronen Palan describes this lack of intervention as follows: 'It seems they [the Bank of England and bankers] reached an agreement – never written down – if a bank intermediated between two non-residents in a foreign currency (in this case the dollar) then this particular deal will not be considered by the Bank of England under its own jurisdiction'. It became accepted that the banks' Eurodollar accounts were 'elsewhere' and therefore the Bank of England had no responsibility for regulating them.

And this is how we arrive at dear little Guernsey, which was to become 'elsewhere' or 'offshore'. How that came about is the next step in the story.

Several critics of the financial services industry maintain that the City of London became nervous at the origins of some of their Eurodollars. The City recognised they were indeed a little too warm for comfort, but nevertheless still wanted the money to flow into their UK banks, so that loans could be made at profitable rates.

Our anti-City of London critics claim what happened next was that the banks found a way to take the business 'offshore' pretty much literally, by creating a series of what they called 'secrecy

7: OFFSHORE OR OFFSIDE?

jurisdictions' from where the dollars could be received and then quietly funnelled back through to the City of London. The Cayman Islands were the first such secrecy jurisdiction. According to *The Spider's Web*: 'Accountants and lawyers arrived and drafted a number of secrecy laws and regulations'.

At this point, I should point out the use of the word 'secrecy' is a pretty emotional term and I know that those working for the Crown Dependencies and Overseas Territories like Guernsey would dispute the quote from *The Spider's Web* and talk about the difference between 'confidentiality' and 'secrecy'. The Crown Dependencies all base their legal systems and legislation on the same common law system as operates in the United Kingdom and would counter the words of *The Spider's Web* by saying that they do not have statute law which imposes secrecy provisions, but that clients are protected by confidentiality obligations under common law.

Back to *The Spiders Web*, where Professor Palan noted that even where tax havens started out as 'trading centres', they can eventually become 'captured' by 'powerful foreign finance and legal firms who write the laws of these countries which they then exploit'.[15]

The so-called secrecy benefits written into their laws immediately attracted a lot of capital into the Cayman Islands which, according to author of *Treasure Islands*, Nicolas Shaxson, came from 'straightforward illegal activity'.[16]

It was clear that the Bank of England knew what was going on in the Caribbean, as can be seen from a secret Bank report dated 11 April 1969, and quoted in *The Spider's Web*:

> We need to be quite sure that the possible proliferation of trust companies, banks etc, which in most cases would be no more than brass plates manipulating assets outside the islands, does not get out of hand. There is of course no objection to

their providing boltholes for non-residents, but we need to be quite sure that in so doing opportunities are not created for the transfer of UK capital to the non-sterling area outside UK rules.

Of the 14 Crown Dependencies and Overseas Territories that Britain had after Suez, seven became tax havens and included the Cayman Islands, Bermuda, the British Virgin Islands, as well as Jersey and Guernsey. Each offered 'secrecy' or common law confidentiality, each provided branches of European banks and each had a plethora of advisors ready to help set up trusts. And of course, the money in these funds would then be channelled back into the City, from their offshore branches and used as loan financing. It should be noted that Guernsey did not specifically pass any laws designed to attract financial services business, as the relevant conditions already existed.

It was these trust funds that became the instrument used in secrecy jurisdictions, to manage the money flowing into the offshore banks. As noted earlier, trusts involve an owner of assets putting that asset into the hands of trustees, who then invest the assets for whoever the original owner nominates. They are called trusts, as the owner of the assets put their trust in the person or entity into which they transfer their ownership. Trusts could hide their ownership, they were not regulated, and there were no annual statements of performance. Today things have been tightened up, and trustees are now regulated by the Guernsey Financial Services Commission (GFSC).

There were clearly benefits for individuals to put their money offshore, but also for UK banks. If questions were asked about the money, the banks and UK government would say that they could do little about its origins, as that was the purview of the local jurisdiction, over which they had no control.

Ultimately this conspiracy theory reflects a simple reality of the second half of the twentieth century, which is well expressed by Ronen Palan: '[Tax havens] are the direct outcome of the conflicting principles of national sovereignty in an age of mobile capital'.[17]

There we are – two possible ways in which the financial services industry got started in Guernsey. One view is a bottom-up story of individuals seeking ways to minimise taxation and the other – a top-down story of the City of London preserving its power by creating so-called secrecy jurisdictions offshore into which Eurodollars flowed. One happened by accident and the other by design.

Guernsey Financial Services - Accident or Not?

So, was the birth of this key new industry by design or accident? My inclination is to see it as accidental. And certainly, the States seemed to reflect this viewpoint in their 'Outside Development Plan' prepared in 1967. This talked a lot about the 'two main props of the economy – Horticulture and Tourism' and then almost as an aside mentions a third source 'the resident immigrant or rentier and, on a larger scale, the locally registered commercial companies and finance houses from outside'.[18]

It goes on to say that 'large sums of outside money and local money are handled, which creates profits and income which in turn provides a considerable source of revenue'. Then after making this point, the States admits 'no information is available as to the sums involved' and reinforces this lack of knowledge by saying 'the money imported by the rentiers and locally registered companies from outside is not known to the Committee, but it is apparent that in terms of direct and indirect taxation accruing to the economy, it forms an economic factor of considerable importance'.

This all seems very reminiscent of the surprise the States felt when it realised how important the stone export market was for the island one hundred years earlier. This naivety about the early success of financial services suggests it was mostly outside forces that created the new industry, rather than a deliberate effort on behalf of the local politicians. As Tony Gallienne reflected in his book *Guernsey in the 21st Century*: 'finance business came to the island without the island really trying'.[19]

And this idea of Guernsey becoming an offshore financial centre 'without really trying' has some further credibility by thinking about the infrastructure needed for such an industry. Clients need to get to the island to look their advisors in the eyes. They need to stay overnight somewhere. They want to have something decent to eat. Airports, hotels, restaurants all need building. And luckily for Guernsey, all these things already existed – thanks to the tourist industry. As Mark Hampton and John Christensen note, the Guernsey financial services industry 'got a free ride because the infrastructure was already in place'.[20]

These two authors make another relevant point. All those wealthy rentiers who came to the island, either for retirement or to avoid the UK tax regime, had the need for what they call a 'pinstripe infrastructure' – banks, accountants, lawyers, financial advisors and managers. So even before the first merchant bank waded ashore in St Peter Port, there were professionals available to be hired and put to use by the *rentiers* who became the industry pathfinders.

A final point, supporting this sleepwalking into an offshore finance centre, comes from the author Ronan Palan who notes:

> Modern tax havens did not originate as part of a conscious .... strategy. Rather they evolved slowly and haphazardly; [they] appeared to have stumbled upon the various attributes of tax havens.[21]

Financial Services: The Growth Years

If we see the 60s as the birth of financial services on the island, then the next three decades represent the growth years of the industry. There are five big parts of financial services – banking, insurance, trusts, funds and support services. The industry has had an extraordinary impact on the lives of every Guernsey man and woman, not least in their pockets with Guernsey's economy growing often at twice the rate of the mainland.

Banks

As we noted earlier, financial services covers not just commercial banking, but many other services. However, the starting point must be the banks, because this is a key portal through which money arrives in Guernsey. So let's look at what's happened to banks in the island.

Guernsey's first bank was established by Thomas Priaulx, and started issuing its own bank notes in 1827, based on privateers' money. It was known as the Guernsey Old Bank, and remained independent until 1924, when it was acquired by the National Provincial and Union, which in turn became the NatWest in 1970. The Old Bank was joined on the High Street in St Peter Port and St Sampson's by the other four familiar UK clearing banks, and the island existed as a sort of banking backwater until 1963, when the first merchant bank arrived on the island.

What triggered the first merchant bank to set up a base in St Peter Port? One of the reasons has been mentioned already; British colonies around the world were increasingly exposed to local governments becoming more adept at taxation.

The first merchant bank to set up shop in the Channel Islands (in Jersey) was probably the Royal Trust of Canada (according to

David Hinshaw,[22] who ran Kleinwort Benson for 30 years).

It's probable that the Royal Trust of Canada arrived in Jersey at a time when the company were becoming increasingly worried about the security of the bank's interests in the Caribbean. This was because in the early 60s, the economies in that region were suffering, plus independence movements started restricting bank business. So it made sense to move sterling to the tranquil shores of the Channel Islands.

This same story was echoed in the arrival of Guernsey's first merchant bank – Kleinwort Benson – which opened for business in a small set of offices in Berthelot Street, off the High Street in St Peter Port in 1963. The origins of the Guernsey office start with this established London bank forming an exotically-named joint venture called the Arawak Trust Company in the 50s, through which they serviced clients in the West Indies. Just like their Canadian counterpart, they grew worried about the likely consequences of the local independence movements and looked for a safe haven for their sterling deposits – and that came to mean the Channel Islands.

The first manager of Kleinwort Benson in Guernsey was Stewart Faulkner, who we met earlier in this chapter. An Ulsterman who had spent his early career as a tax official in Malaysia and Singapore, and who then took a post with the States of Guernsey as an inspector of taxes. This eventually bored him and although he'd never run a bank, his colonial credentials clearly impressed head office in London, who gave him the chance to run this new outpost of the business.

And it was the colonial money that Stewart Faulkner was able to attract that built the Kleinwort Benson business in Guernsey. Much of it came from East Africa as we mentioned earlier, which was opened up by the completion of the East African Railway in 1906, joining the port of Mombasa with the fertile highlands of Kenya and led, according to Kenya-advisor.com, to: 'Thousands of white settlers (coming) in to establish coffee, tobacco and tea plantations'. These were joined, in the colonies of Kenya and Rhodesia amongst others, by ex-soldiers who had been given land grants after World War 1. By 1961, the white farming community consisted of some 2,700 families who occupied 16,700 square miles of land and had become rich from huge farms that grew and exported tea and cotton to the UK. Their efforts were supported by a large infrastructure, managed by many of the 30,000 settlers who came to live in the region at the end of World War 2.

In 1960, the economic survey of the Nairobi government estimated that Kenyan agricultural revenue in 1959 was the equivalent of over £800 million (at 2021 rates). Local farmers' accountants had them invest this sterling-based wealth in stocks and shares, and then recommended them to place these assets in discretionary trusts, run by (amongst others) Kleinwort Benson.

This kind of protective financial shield around the colonist's assets was something the clearing banks did not offer. Kleinwort Benson had a whole suite of options (call accounts, seven-day deposits, monthly fixed deposits, etc) that were light years ahead of the dusty, stuck in their ways, clearing banks up the High Street in St Peter Port. Guernsey's first merchant bank really benefited from colonial farmers and their accountants, who saw Guernsey 'as a safe place for their assets outside the UK where it would have been taxed even as non-residents', according to Keith Corbin (who was recruited by Stewart Faulkner after he embarked on his next merchant bank establishment in Guernsey, Slater Walker).[23]

Not only was their wealth protected by secretive trusts, they also would only pay 20% income tax if they were tax resident in Guernsey, because of the States reduction in this tax in 1962. (Trust beneficiaries who were not residents in Guernsey would not be subject to local income tax). It makes me think that Guernsey's reduction in income tax may have acted as a public relations spark. It brought a sudden greater awareness of the attractiveness of the island to non-resident, high net-worth individuals.

Of course, the immediate success of Kleinwort Benson Guernsey led to other merchant banks appearing on the island. Stewart Faulkner himself traded on this growth, by moving on to open a branch of Rothschild in the island and then, in the early 70s, an office for Slater Walker.

Clearly there were enough British colonists around the world to fund the early growth of merchant banks in Guernsey. But another group of investors started to take an interest in the attractive tax regime of Guernsey. The globalisation of international commerce had begun to make multinational organisations far less rooted in their original homes. They had become stateless, and financial directors of these multinationals began to see the benefits of a regime like Guernsey. Why not set up a company in Guernsey? There would be no capital gains tax, no corporation tax, and no income tax if no business was conducted on the island. But to do so, they needed help to create a Guernsey-based company – and that's what merchant banks do.

This kind of thinking was new at the start of the 60s. It reflected a more global approach by big companies, who would set up production wherever the cheapest labour could be had. But that meant paying for the construction of factories or for extraction of minerals and ores all over the world. The big companies needed loans to pay for these investments. Unfortunately for them, local governments were dead set against their currency leaving the country and so imposed laws to prevent it happening.

And that's when the Eurocurrency market came into play – or, as already discussed, the Eurodollar market. Guernsey had access to the Eurocurrency market and that meant offshore companies could access the money they needed to expand their operations without the interference of their home market legislators. This was indeed the beginning of what came to be called 'the internationalisation of capital'.

The merchant banks would get income by setting up companies on the island and advising organisations on financial matters. They would also be getting large sums of money coming into their banks from their multinational clients, which could then be channelled back to the UK, where high interest rates were available on Eurocurrency deposits and low interest rates on Eurocurrency loans. There was money to be made here.

We could say that the arrival of the first merchant bank on the streets of St Peter Port was the start of the island as an offshore financial centre. This idea of an offshore financial centre was defined by RA Johns in 1983 as follows: 'A small territory in which the conduct of international banking business is facilitated by favourable and/or flexibly administered tax, exchange control and banking laws and in which the volume of banking business is totally unrelated to the size and needs of the domestic market'.[24]

Guernsey's attractive tax regime was also appealing to what are known as High or Ultra High Net Worth individuals. These were the entrepreneurs who benefitted from the boom in global business in the 60s and for whom the extremely high rates of taxes in the UK were an anathema. They were joined by people of inherited wealth.

These wealthy individuals started bringing their money to the island, particularly to avoid death duties in the UK, which rose from 50% on an estate of £100,000, to 80% on an estate worth £1 million or more. To put this in perspective, in 2022 a UK citizen pays no inheritance tax on an estate of £350,000 or less, or potentially up to £1 million, once married parents and family homes are involved. So, in the 60s, rates could be double this and thus made setting up home in Guernsey an attractive proposition, as Guernsey had a zero rate of death duties.

Not wishing to miss out on this new financial action, other merchant banks started appearing on the streets of Guernsey's main town and, by 1975, a first banking peak was reached with over 40 banks ready to accept money from all over the world. If you look at the Guernsey telephone directories from 1975, you'll see just in that one year, ten new merchant banks appearing and offering their services to the public, including the Bank of Bermuda, the First National Bank of Boston, the Italian International Bank and the Manufacturers Hanover Corporation.

David Hinshaw reckons that in addition to other merchant banks piling into the island, they were joined in this period by UK building societies who wanted some of this new action. Most of them didn't really thrive, apart from the Skipton and Yorkshire Building Societies.

This early banking growth was fuelled by the UK government, who introduced different legislative roadblocks to halt their loss of control over tax income. First came the Capital Gains Tax in 1965/66, which interested parties overcame with the establishment of trusts, with the help of the experts in the merchant banks. Then came the negotiations to join the European Common Market, which required the UK to shrink the sterling area (the territory within which the pound was the effective currency). Suddenly, a lot of Caribbean banks found their clients leaving to protect their sterling funds. The EU negotiations were also positive for Guernsey in 1973, in that Protocol 3 confirmed the preservation of the island's fiscal autonomy.

By 1975, these UK government activities resulted in about 40 banks offering their services in St Peter Port and jostling for clients from all over the world. Guernsey's financial neighbour Jersey, also helped, due to a panic there about population growth and worries about the economy overheating. In 1972, they introduced a moratorium on banks opening and this led to at least six banks coming to Guernsey instead.[25] This ban lasted until 1976.

Finally, in this early growth period, further positive impetus to bank profitability came in 1979 from the removal of exchange controls. Exchange control meant that UK residents – individuals and companies – were prohibited from holding foreign currencies or securities quoted on foreign stock exchanges. The regulation's purpose was to help the authorities conserve the gold and foreign currency reserves and maintain the UK's balance of payment positions. By eliminating this tight government control, international capital movement was freed up and helped the birth of the globalisation of business. The removal of exchange controls meant that money could flow freely in and out of the sterling area, and so allowed the island to develop a multi-currency service.[26] This in turn helped institutions develop their trust operations.[27]

This relaxation of control became the precursor for the famous 'Big Bang' – the City of London financial sector reform in 1986. This deregulated the convoluted activity of buying or selling shares, and led to banks suddenly being able to own stockbrokers and jobbing firms. Fixed rate commissions were removed, foreign companies were allowed into the City and electronic trading began.

The number of banks in Guernsey remained pretty static until the late 80s, when another boom led to a jump from 40 banks up to 70 by 1990, and to 79 by 1999, which was the high water mark of Guernsey's bank saturation.[28]

The Big Bang, plus the general globalisation of capital movement and business in general, led to the arrival of many non-UK banks into the island. The Guernsey 'brand' became far more well-known across the globe, and thanks to mergers and acquisitions, large numbers of foreign banks arrived – for example the Bank of Yokohama, which had acquired the London bank Guinness Mahon, and Deutsche Bank, which had bought Morgan Grenfell.

Too Many Banks?

From this highpoint at the end of the 20th century, began a continuous decline to just 20 banks by 2020. In reality, at the start of the 21st century, Guernsey was truly 'over-banked'. This led to a fight for business and an inevitable decline in profit margins. Consolidation of banks started to take place to reduce overheads, and banks began to see that power was moving east, which led to a migration from western financial centres like Guernsey. In addition, new jurisdictions began to compete with Guernsey and introduced new products to steal business from the merchant banks in the High Street.

The Global Economic Crisis in 2008 exacerbated the decline. The crisis was caused by US banks initially lending sub-optimal mortgages, and then selling their mortgage books to banks around the world. The defaulting of these mortgages led to banks taking possession of properties with negative equity. To compensate, head offices started pulling back money from their offshore branches to shore up their businesses. This 'upstreaming money' strategy hit Guernsey hard.

Another stab in the back for Guernsey-based banks was the idea amongst US banks with subsidiaries in Guernsey that there was something disreputable about offshore financial centres, and that they shouldn't be associated with them. And then secondly, after Brexit in 2016, European banks started feeling it was not right to have branches in this new EU-rejecting jurisdiction. So, in 20 years, Guernsey lost nearly 60 banks.

Of course, some exits were due to consolidation, or to a realisation that a local office often just duplicated cost. Was this because less money was being put on deposit? At first sight it appears not. Money held in the island's banks rose from £15 billion in 1990, to £104 billion in 2020. But looking a bit closer,

7: Offshore Or Offside?

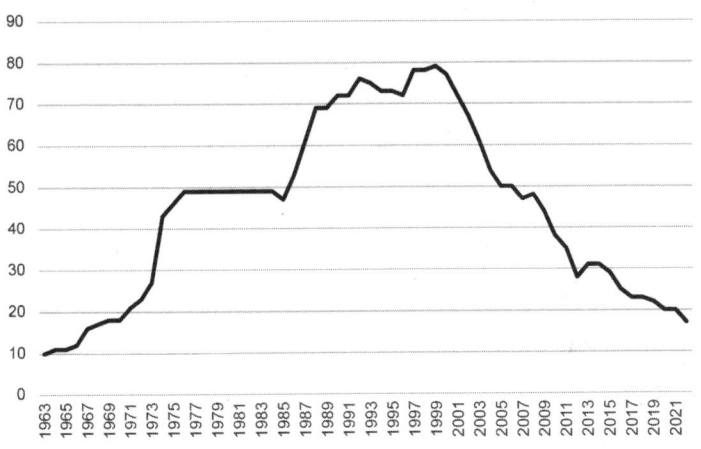

Fig 6: Number of Banks, 1963–2021.
(See Appendix for sources)

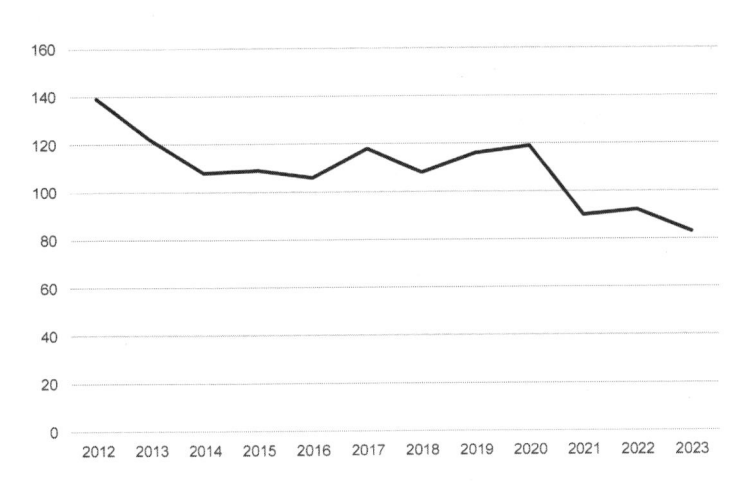

Fig 7: Bank Deposits (£bn), 2012–2023.
(See Appendix for sources)

reworking all the deposits at 2020 values; we can see that from a peak in 2009, the true value of deposits has dropped back to pre-2000 levels (See Fig. 7).

Beyond Banking

If the Guernsey banks made winners out of individuals and corporations who put their money into local coffers, there were also losers. Unfortunately for the Guernsey banks, these losers were national governments, whose politicians became increasingly irritated with this little island.

And so began a cat-and-mouse game that has lasted from the 60s right up to the present day. As Guernsey attracted more money from wealthy individuals and corporations, so national governments legislated to make this exodus harder and harder. As Philip Marr, economist with the Guernsey Financial Services Commission, noted in a speech: 'The International Community kept moving the regulatory goal posts'.[29] These same international communities not only produced financial roadblocks with their legislation, they also undermined investor confidence in places like Guernsey, by the constant drip-feed of negative publicity about the financial sector's integrity, and depicting customers of Guernsey's attractive tax situation as undesirables.

What could the island do against this constant battering from governments around the world? The main response has been diversification – offering new services that spread the risk of losing the lucrative inflow of money. It would seem that Guernsey had finally learned the lesson of all the previous chapters in this book – don't bet all your money on one horse – spread the risk. Of course, this is much easier with an industry that requires brains rather than quarries, hotels or greenhouses.

The rest of this chapter will be taken up with looking at

the different ways the Guernsey financial services industry has diversified to maintain its position in the world's money markets.

Trusts

Imagine you are a wealthy farmer in Kenya in 1963, and have just heard that the UK government has decided to give the colony its independence. You'd be more than a bit worried about what's going to happen to your savings and what restrictions will be placed on passing on your wealth to your children.

Over drinks, at say, the Kenya Regiment Club in Nairobi, you start talking to a representative of Kleinwort Benson, who drops in every few months looking for business. They suggest you move your sterling to Guernsey where you'll earn good interest, tax free. So, you follow their advice and now you have your assets safely stored away in a little island off the coast of France.

But could you do more with this money? In particular, could you safeguard your children's inheritance? This is where merchant banks like Kleinwort Benson opened a second area of activity – with trusts. Originally a scheme created in the Middle Ages to protect the wives and children of crusaders, trusts have become a large part of the Guernsey offshore finance industry.

A quick bit of terminology explanation. A 'trustor' or 'settlor' is the person or company that sets up a trust, passing ownership of their wealth to a 'trustee' who is the person or company that administers the trust on behalf of the trustor.

There are several potential benefits of trusts which can include the following. First of all, they are secret and the trustor's name is never revealed. Second, as the trustor no longer owns the funds in the trust, they are not subject to death duties or inheritance tax. Thirdly, the trust system makes it easier to have a more flexible approach to the use of the assets by the beneficiaries, compared to the legal obligations of a will. Fourthly, the trustor's assets are protected from creditors because the money is now owned by a third party – the trustee. And fifthly, having a trust with clear instructions on how the assets are to be distributed, ensures a quick benefit to the beneficiaries compared to going through probate, which can be a slow process to decide who gets what. The trust terms ensure that the trustors wishes are met – even beyond the grave.

But perhaps the best reason for choosing to create a trust can be found in the actual word 'trust'. Trust implies that one person trusts another not to let them down and, in the case of trusts, that person is what's called a fiduciary – the trustee that administers a trust, and they are bound by fiduciary duties. To quote an observation made by the offshore law firm Carey Olsen:

> A trustee may not be released from the duty to act in the best interests of the beneficiaries of a trust and this is the principal reason to choose the trust over other tools for wealth management.[30]

And to quote another source, it has been said that fiduciaries: 'must be worthy of being trusted to the ends of the earth, no matter what difficulties they may face'.[31]

No pressure there then!

Guernsey has been a serious location for trusts since the early 60s and was specifically mentioned by Kleinwort Benson's original manager, Stewart Faulkner in the Open University TV programme from 1975. He noted: 'The next stage of development would probably [have been] the introduction of capital gains tax in the UK around 1965/66, [which] meant a fair amount of trusts were set up in the Channel Islands for UK settlors, UK residents and a number of existing settlements were transferred from the UK to the Channel Islands'.[32]

Since those early beginnings, the number of licensed fiduciaries handling trusts in Guernsey has grown significantly and there have been around 150 licensees since 2012. These professionals and their companies have seen their turnover grow in the 21st century, from around £150 million per year in 2005, to £350 million in 2020, and employs just over 3,000 local people – around 10% of the island's total workforce.[33]

The trusts handled by the Guernsey fiduciaries vary a lot. Back in the 60s it would have been wealthy families who established trusts, to ensure smooth succession planning and responsible asset management. But through the decades, the fiduciary industry has developed a number of innovations to grow their businesses. Pension funds have established trusts to ensure correct financial management of their assets and, more recently, Guernsey offices in the Gulf States have been able to attract special Islamic-law-based trusts for wealthy people in this region.

This labour-intensive sector of the finance industry on the island now administers 20,000 trusts according to globalbanks.com.

Funds

Let's go back again to 1963: the arrival of the first merchant bank on the island and that farmer from Kenya who moved their money into a trust for their children. They would have expected the fiduciary who managed the trust to make sure the money in the trust grows. Bank interest rates at the start of the 60s in the UK were around 5% and so our settlor would be agitating for the trustee to do better – perhaps by buying stocks and shares in various blue-chip companies. But shares in companies can go down in value as well as up.

Is there a safer way to make such investments? Well, yes, there is. And Guernsey has become a major player in what are known as investment funds. This financial vehicle first started back in the 18th century in Holland, where its creator, Adriaan van Ketwich, opened a fund for investors with limited capital who wanted a safe way to grow their money, based on the motto 'Unity creates strength'. And that pretty much sums up the benefits of investment funds, even today.

The modern investment fund, still based on Ketwich's original principles, offers a small investor the chance to join with other similar punters to pool their money into a fund, professionally administered by investment experts, and buy shares in a diverse range of companies. This range could be either across many industries and geographies or focused on one sector in particular. The wide range of the portfolio means a reduction in risk and the pooling of resources provides economies of scale when it comes to the cost of administering the fund.

If the economy is doing well and companies are profitable, the fund can provide a better return than bank interest. Equally, in a depressed economy, funds won't be as attractive. Indeed, there is a correlation between bank interest rates and the performance of funds. So in the 60s and 70s, when interest rates were no higher than 8%, this investment vehicle did well. But then in the 80s and 90s, with interest rates up at just under 15%, they were less successful – challenged by less vulnerable insurance policies with a guaranteed interest rate after a certain period. Since the beginning of the new century, with interest rates often under one percent, funds have again become an attractive proposition, especially with a generally positive economy (excluding the crash of 2008).

There are two main types of investment funds: 'open-ended funds' and 'closed-ended funds'. The open-ended version doesn't have a fixed number of shares and can shrink or grow based on demand. They are attractive because an investor can get their money out whenever they want by redeeming their shares through the fund manager.

The closed ended variety is different. A once-only issuing of a defined number of shares happens at an Initial Public Offering (IPO) and then gets traded on the stock market or can remain unlisted, if the initial investors choose to do so. Closed funds tend to contain companies whose assets are illiquid, like property – things that cannot be sold at the clicking of fingers.

Guernsey has become a serious contender in the global funds market. Supporters point to a credible regulatory regime which combines flexibility and competitiveness, plus an easily understood simplicity for setting up new funds. And this flexibility means trust managers and other investors can be quite creative, so for example they were amongst the first to invest in Indian companies after liberalisation by their government in 1993. It should also be noted that Guernsey funds impose no income tax, no VAT, no capital gains tax and no inheritance tax.

In 2022, the island's fund administrators handled 139 open-ended funds, with assets of £51 billion, and 829 close-ended funds with assets of £241 billion.[34] Since 2013, the number of open-ended funds has dropped, whilst close-ended funds have grown by nearly a third in the same period. Combining both types of funds, Guernsey administers nearly 1,000 funds with a net asset value of £292 billion – up a third since 2013.

Insurance

In case you've forgotten, Guernsey is a tiny island of 24 square miles with a population of around 60,000. So, it's not big in global terms, you could almost say insignificant but, guess what? In 2020, it was the world's leading centre for non-US and International captive insurance companies. More than 20% of the UK FTSE 100 have captive insurance companies domiciled in the island.[35]

You are probably now asking yourself: 'what on earth is a captive insurance company and why are there so many in Guernsey?' Let's start by talking about your own insurance policies. You have probably got car insurance, travel insurance and house insurance. Why? Well because you know that things can go wrong in each of these areas and when they do, they cost a lot of money to put right. So you pay an annual premium for the insurance company to take on that risk. This logic also applies to commercial companies. They have risks in their daily operations and want to avoid expensive solutions. To do so, they also take out insurance policies.

Now back to you for a moment. When you get your renewal notices from your insurance companies, I bet there's often a deep intake of breath and a moan about how much your premium has gone up. Again, it's the same for big companies. This though is where things are different for you and the big corporations. You can shop around a bit, but that's all you can do. Companies can do something else. They can start their own insurance company, pay annual premiums to it and have much more control over costs, over red tape and bureaucracy and over what risks they want to cover. They could also build up reserves over time and, as they were based in Guernsey, paid no or lower taxes on their profits.

These insurance businesses that companies set up are called 'captive insurance' and were named by an American insurance broker called Frederick M Reiss, who had the idea to help an Ohio manufacturing company client with several of its own mines. He wanted to not only set up a captive insurance subsidiary for them to reduce costs, but also to make it as tax efficient as possible.

Clever Mr Reiss decided to take advantage of Bermuda's closeness to the US mainland, its stable government and its low tax regime. So that's where his clients' captive insurance company was set up. He could now get the parent company to pay premiums to the Bermuda-based organisation, claim tax relief on the premiums in the high tax US mainland, and pay no or low tax on any profits of the subsidiary in its offshore domicile.

In a nutshell, captive insurance companies can help organisations avoid paying high premiums to outside insurance firms. They can insure risks that outside operators might hesitate to support, can cut through the long lead times to be paid on any claim, and can benefit from any profit the subsidiary might make by locating in tax advantageous locations.

A final benefit of captive insurance is that the company's own in-house insurance set-up may not want to take on all the risk of the policy and so, because it is an official insurance company, it can pass on some of that risk to an outside insurance organisation. This is called reinsurance and there are numerous companies who just do this.

So that's how reinsurance started and now we come to the involvement of Guernsey. In the late 60s and early 70s, many large organisations started to see what was happening in America with offshore captive insurance and began to start their own versions. Although pioneered in the 1920s by companies like ICI and Unilever, captive insurance companies really took off towards the last quarter of the 20th century. Mark Hampton estimates there were 1,955 captives worldwide in 1989, which increased to 2,568 by 1993.[36] This growth has continued into the 21st century, with Guernsey alone the home of over 200 captives.[37]

For UK and European companies, the leading captives' homes of Bermuda and the Cayman Islands were a long way away, and in a different time zone. Closer to hand was Guernsey. An island already successfully handling international finance through its local banking subsidiaries and therefore full of smart, finance-savvy personnel. It was an island with a low-tax regime and quite simple laws for commercial operations. And, most importantly, an island government who could see the benefits of becoming the captive insurance domicile for UK and European companies – unlike their rival, Jersey, in the 1970s who had a law in place prohibiting the creation of captive insurance arrangements.

Sadly, we can't identify the smoking gun that started things off but, from around 1970, Guernsey began attracting large numbers of insurance organisations. And by that time the States had learned the lessons of the early 60s, when they had no control or understanding of the value of the banking industry. So, in 1969, the States passed a law limiting the use of the word 'insurance' in the title of any new company being set up. This enabled the States, right from the beginning, to control the growth of this new sector. And this was reinforced by a second law passed in 1986, to further tighten control over the rapid expansion of captive insurance companies.

A 1987 Peat Marwick report entitled 'An Economic Appraisal of Guernsey', commissioned by the States, revealed that Guernsey at that time was the third largest home for captive insurance companies in the world, after Bermuda and the Cayman Islands.[38] By 2008, the island was the fourth biggest captive insurance domicile in the world, and at the start of 2023, Guernsey was the largest domicile for captive insurance in Europe.

To give you some idea of the scale of the risks these Guernsey-based captive insurance companies underwrote, consider the case of BP. They had their own captive in Guernsey called Jupiter Insurance. Unfortunately, in 2010, a BP-managed oil rig in the Gulf of Mexico leaked, resulting in the largest marine oil spill in history. Jupiter stumped up $700 million as part of a compensation package demanded by US courts. It sounds a lot, but this figure was just Jupiter's maximum policy limit. BP itself will end up paying many billions of dollars, as Jupiter did not share the policy risk by going on to the reinsurance market (BP had decided its own coffers were deep enough). This was quite unusual as most captives limit their risk to around $100 to $200 million and go to the reinsurance market for the rest.

And just to throw around a few more mind-boggling figures, Jupiter made an underwriting profit of $1.68 billion in 2011, and had a $7.9 billion asset base. This asset base is the money Jupiter had available to invest and make profits to pay for any policy claims. In their case, they provided some of this money as loans back to its parent company.

Now back to our captive insurance history. The enormous growth of the captive insurance business in Guernsey attracted the envy of other low tax regimes and, bit by bit, other domiciles muscled in on the action. The Isle of Man, Luxembourg, Ireland, even Holland, all have taken market share, but little Guernsey has maintained its buoyancy – by innovating.

It does now get a bit complicated – but stay with me. In 1997, Guernsey created a new type of captive insurance structure called the Protected Cell Company (PCC) or Segregated Portfolio Company (SPC). The first one was Aon's White Rock Insurance company, PCC Ltd.

The PCC business organisation structure comprises a core and radiating cells around the core. Initially, the idea was that each cell represented a different policy (fire, health, auto, life, etc), and its assets are only those related to the particular risk being covered. Very quickly this new cell structure was extended from insurance to individual assets of a company. The benefit of having individual cells is that in insolvency, creditors can only get money back from a specific cell rather than clawing back from all the cells. Equally, income tax demands on profits from one cell do not impact different tax demands on other cells. The 'core' of a PCC handles all administration issues for all cells, and this reduces overhead costs for each one. It also maintains the minimum capital required by local regulations. PCCs have become popular around the world and over 100 corporations now use this type of structure.

What does the future look like for captive insurance in Guernsey? Well, the world is certainly becoming an increasingly tricky place for companies to do business with high inflation, disrupted supply chains, climate change and low economic growth. This all ramps up the risks for organisations and the cost for insuring against this uncertainty. No wonder that numbers of captive insurance companies now exceed traditional insurers. Given all this, the future looks encouraging for in-house insurance. Will it also be positive for Guernsey? The island is certainly facing more competition from other offshore centres but, set against that, Guernsey has stability, a good regulatory body and 100 years of experience in this form of risk management.

Support Services

We have covered the four big parts of Guernsey's financial services, but there is a growing, almost anonymous, fifth leg to this industry. More than 50 years of activity has created a local army of outsourced, highly skilled, experienced support personnel: recruitment, IT, PR, and many more. Accountants flourish on the island in a profusion that recalls memories of the tomato industry. And in particular, we should point out the growth of specialist lawyers (called advocates in Guernsey). In 1970, there were just 11 advocates on the island, whilst today there are 24 law firms, each with their own advocates, amounting in total to 221 practising professionals (as of July 2023), interpreting the law of the island for the banks, trusts, funds, captive insurance companies and their clients. In 2020, the States reckoned this support services group represented 13% of Guernsey's labour market.

Financial Services Future

Guernsey's finance industry grew from delivering 7% of the island's economy (GDP) in 1971, to 65% in 2001. The 2007–8 global financial crisis hit the industry hard, but from 2011 onwards, it has contributed around 40% of Guernsey's income. Similarly with employment, the number of people in the industry reached a peak in 2007, with 25% of the working population employed in the finance sector and is now around 20%.

Today the split of activity within the finance industry is first: trusts, with 29% of all employed; then banking with 28%; in third place, funds, with 22% of all workers; and insurance with 13%. The total is completed with around 8% of finance industry employees coming from a mixed group of brokerage activities and money service providers.[39]

So yes, the finance sector is still incredibly important to the island's economy but are we seeing, like with all our previous industries, a slide into late maturity and eventual disappearance? Some would see the finance industry as a continuation of all the industries on the island that came before it. This has been nicely put by Tony Gallienne: 'For all its alien strangeness … finance represents something which is no different to what Guernsey has been doing since 1204 – taking advantage of its autonomous position, making its own laws and setting its own taxes, in such a way as to make a living'.[40]

Compared to all our other chapters, finance has demonstrated strong innovative tendencies and has risen to the challenge that every UK, EU or global body has thrown at it. It has reacted quickly to tackling money laundering and terrorist financing as required by the FATF (Financial Action Task Force). It shows commitment to sharing information. And it has given its full support to transparency as required by the G20, OECD and the EU.

In addition to the industry's positive attitude towards innovation and broadening its base, the States has also shown a willingness to try new ways of diversification. In 2016 they created Locate Guernsey to attract new business and individuals, and has invested in the Digital Greenhouse to try and grow the digital and creative sectors. The local government has also made investments to help build the island's green finance initiatives, and in 2018, the island introduced the world's first green fund product.[41]

The island's finance industry is also different from preceding industries like tourism, stone export and tomato growing in that it has diversified into four distinct sub-sectors – banking, trusts, funds and insurance. This certainly gives it some balance with some doing better than others at different times. So there may be fewer banks today, but fiduciary licenses remain stable and so does their income.

Despite all these positive points, the attack on offshore finance centres like Guernsey by major governments and institutions appears relentless, particularly after the crash of 2008. And despite the nimbleness of the States in demonstrating a willingness to answer many of the issues raised by opponents of the offshore industry, this 'chasing the artful dodger' as David Richardson called it in 2019, seems to be building even more momentum.[42] The world's press is full of extraordinary statistics that place Guernsey and others in an unattractive light, as can be seen below:

'Governments currently lose around $240 billion pa through tax avoidance'.[43]

'Half the world's trade appears to pass through tax havens, although they account for only 3% of the world's GDP'.[44]

'Zucman (2013) estimates that about 6% of global households' financial wealth ($7.6 trillion) is held in tax havens'.[45]

Against this flood of negative statistics, there has been a push-back from the local finance industry with many positive statistics about the benefits for Guernsey. But the fact remains that the island's biggest earner is under more sustained attack than it has ever faced before.

So we come to the ultimate question. Will the island have to reinvent itself yet again? You would hope that academics could come to the rescue with untainted analyses on this industry. Sadly, there has been very little proper independent research – according to a study in 2017, only 0.4% of academic literature is on taxation.[46]

The local industry itself still has great confidence in its future. A 2023 survey by Guernsey Finance shows two-thirds of its members expressed confidence in the sector's future.[47] And the figures from the States seem to confirm that the Guernsey finance industry 'brand' has remained a steady 40% of total GDP in the first two decades of the 21st century.

Of course, Guernsey finance and the States clearly have a great need to big-up this part of the economy. But are there signs that this current Guernsey brand could go the way of their previous six brand compatriots?

I want to use banks as a way of testing the health of the finance industry, because they are, in many respects, the portal into the broader offshore finance business. The island is currently home to around 20 banks, down from 79 in 1999. That's a drop of three quarters in less than 25 years. Some of this shrinkage is down to consolidation, but it's also true that banking is going through some really hard times. Interest rates are very low, which impacts profitability and makes consumers hesitant about using them as an investment vehicle. If you want to put Euros, or Swiss francs into the bank, they are going to charge you a negative interest rate and demand a fairly hefty minimum deposit before taking on your business. The bank may also ask you to prove you can provide them with profitable activities through other services. And, specifically related to Guernsey, the high cost of housing rentals, has driven several finance industry employees to give up and relocate, which helps explain the 4.5% drop in sector staff between 2016 and 2022.[48]

One of the early bank arrivals in Guernsey was the Royal Bank of Canada, with a first telephone directory appearance in 1975. In 2019, they downsized from their building in Canada Court to Admiral Park, leaving their spacious offices to the students at Elizabeth College and, in 2023, after nearly 50 years on the island, they announced they were leaving and consolidating their business in Jersey. Their spokesperson told ITV news: 'After carefully considering our current business and operating models in the Channel Islands, we have determined that it is no longer viable to maintain its presence in Guernsey from a scalability, financial and commercial perspective'.[49] In other words, they weren't making any money.

Is the departure of such a long-established bank from the island a one-off? That's certainly the tenor of reactions from the Guernsey authorities. But it's interesting that bank shrinkage is happening all over the world, driven by low interest rates, digitisation and on-line banking and, in general, huge changes in technology that favour the big and hit the also-rans hard. In the United States, one organisation (The Financial Brand Forum) predicts that in America, in the next 20 years, there will be a 54% drop in the number of banks.

Could that happen at the same rate in Guernsey? Could we imagine a finance industry with only ten banks? The differences between offshore finance banks across the world is diminishing, and the examination of their sources of income ever-growing. Could offshore business become ever less viable? It's certain that the island is currently in a high state of anxiety over the forthcoming 2024 inspection by MONEYVAL, whose remit is:

> As a permanent monitoring body of the Council of Europe entrusted with the task of assessing compliance with the principal international standards to counter money laundering and the financing of terrorism and the effectiveness of their implementation, as well as with the task of making recommendations to national authorities in respect of necessary improvements to their systems.[50]

Guernsey is due an audit in 2024, and if the island fails this examination, then it will be put on a grey list and will lose access to some important areas of finance, which in turn will make it less attractive to investors. But the island is using significant resources to ensure they do get a successful outcome which will provide an endorsement of Guernsey's standards of regulation.

Bank departures or consolidations, together with an adverse MONEYVAL inspection, could impact local employment and drive down the importance of the offshore finance industry for the island.

And that's not all the potentially bad news for the finance industry. In 2017, Guernsey signed up to something called the Common Reporting Standard (CRS). This requires the island's financial institutions to identify individuals who are residents for tax in one country, and who have financial accounts in another regime. They are required to pass on all information regarding any offshore accounts to the individuals' home country authorities. Not what an individual trying to avoid tax wants to hear. This does need however to be qualified, as after seven years in operation, this Common Reporting Standard doesn't seem to have impacted very much business.

Nevertheless, the world authorities continue to try to stop or slow down the mobility of business, money and individuals. For example, another piece of legislation also adds to the complexity of being part of the offshore finance industry. This is something called the Global Agreement on Corporate Tax and is a pact between countries that would eliminate a practice that had made Guernsey, amongst others, attractive to big business.

In the past, places like Guernsey were tempting for big corporations to site their head offices, as the island has a zero corporate tax rate. This meant multinationals (particularly in the digital industry) could avoid paying tax on their profits in markets where they did most of their business, and enjoy the zero rate on profits in Guernsey. From 2023, the new agreement enforces a minimum corporate tax rate of at least 15% for multinationals, and requires them to pay tax on profits where they are earned. It's too soon to say what impact this will have on the island, but the signs are ominous.

Finally, a last threat, or opportunity – Artificial Intelligence (AI). There is a certainty that it will replace a lot of jobs in the finance industry which may overcome the perennial Guernsey problem of filling enough industry vacancies and allow staff to concentrate on the personal advice side. There is also the possibility of AI tracking vast amounts of data to identify new customer insights.

What's the prediction – finance industry survival or terminal decline? The statistics on banking don't look good. All over the world banks are suffering – efficiency gains mean fewer staff, low interest rates mean lower profits, retrenchment is now the global norm. And specifically in Guernsey, high living costs are pushing owners of local merchant banks into outsourcing some of the more basic services to cheaper locations. The island also faces the potential negative impact of the Common Reporting Standard which will leave no hiding place for tax dodgers. The Global Agreement on Corporate Tax which will make headquartering in the island less attractive for some global corporations. And finally the 2024 visit of MONEYVAL, which may or may not have implications for the industry.

We've been here before, haven't we? Government legislation negatively impacted the tomato industry, it killed privateering overnight, UK tax changes choked the smuggling business, and the French authorities' actions put an end to the lucrative stockings exports to their market. Will the predatory government 'wolves' circling Guernsey with restrictive legislation, not only impact the banks but also funds, trusts and insurance? It seems likely it will, but the 60 years of knowledge built up by these parts of the industry may provide some protection for them. It may well come down to the issue of tax benefits for all four parts of the industry. If Guernsey finds its tax advantages watered down, will consumers and companies still want to base themselves here?

8: And the Moral of This Story Is?

I began this book by proposing that the history of Guernsey and its economy has been determined by the desires of ordinary people. And I used the term 'consumers' to describe them, as it's my belief that Guernsey has had seven consumer brands that grew, were loved, generated loyalty, but then had this bond eroded by a blindness to changing household needs.

The island's first brand – Guernsey knitwear – might well be recognised as one of the world's first and most long-lasting proprietary names (the 'Guernsey' sweater). The brand grew because the fashion-conscious, middle-class males of France grew tired of saggy, boring blanket cloth hose and embraced the tight, light, colourful and comfortable stockings provided by the wool of England and the dexterity of Guernsey spinsters and knitters.

Guernsey tights were expensive but male peacocks were happy to pay the price for looking good – that is until technology intervened and replaced the unusually clever local spinning wheels and equally adroit spinners with machines that produced a better material, cheaper and quicker. And the French Government also played a role, banning imported knitwear to help nurture their own nascent knitting machine industry. Instead of embracing the new technology, Guernsey reacted by reducing prices and paying the spinners and knitters a lot less, which encouraged the locals to say enough is enough: 'What can we do instead that pays more?'

And so, we come to the island's second brand, that of developing an incredible offshore 'supermarket', full of privateers' plunder. Attracting both legitimate and less honest buyers to the island who, in turn, made desirable treats, such as tea, tobacco and wine, available to households in both the UK and France. The

8: And The Moral Of This Story Is?

island built a fantastic service industry in the 18th century around this, digging cellars for alcohol storage and populating St Peter Port with coopers, carpenters, ship repairers, rope-makers, sail-repairers, hostels, inns and brothels.

Many of the customers arriving in Guernsey at that time were in the smuggling business. They were supplying the ordinary people of the UK and France with goods that were otherwise unaffordable due to the imposition of heavy taxes. Consumers were raising a middle finger to the government and saying the duties on things we want are ridiculous and we won't accept them. And eventually UK politicians got the message. They recognised the large amounts of tax revenue they were losing and started slashing duties firstly on tea and subsequently, under Robert Peel, on hundreds of other luxury items. Smuggling became far less profitable and was reinforced with a succession of anti-smuggling Acts of Parliament at the beginning of the 19th century.

The power of the consumer, demonstrated by the success of smuggling, was given full rein after the Napoleonic Wars, with the death of the mercantile system of protection, imperialism and colonialism and its replacement with a philosophy of free trade. And there was Guernsey ready to build on its success as a middleman. The world and its riches were open. No more pirates or privateers. No need for smuggling. But how to get hold of coffee, tea or textiles? The island's entrepreneurs needed more ships. Which triggered the third Guernsey brand – this time as recognised shipbuilders. It lasted just over 80 years and died with the advent of new steam-powered technology. Wooden ships, in comparison, were too slow, too small and, as a result, their freight too expensive.

Could the Guernsey shipbuilders have done something other than simply waving the white flag? Local shipbuilders would have seen the future from as early as 1843, with the launching of Brunel's wrought iron steamship, the SS *Great Britain*. The artisanal nature of the Guernsey shipyards made a reinvention into the heavy engineering needs of iron ships impossible. There were no iron foundries on the island and importing iron was a lot more expensive than bringing in wood. And all the many handicrafts that had served the island so well were no longer relevant in the age of iron-clad steamship engineering. One must conclude that Guernsey shipbuilders knew their time was up and looked elsewhere for an answer rather than trying to maintain their brand. And the solution lay only a few minutes inland from the shipyards.

Granite quarrying, Guernsey's fourth brand took off as shipbuilding declined, perhaps explaining the nonchalance with which the island took its wooden hulled boat decline. Spurred by the mid 19th century twin explosions of railway construction and urban expansion, Guernsey granite became the go-to brand for hard-wearing foundations for steam train tracks and suburban pavements and roads.

Its demise came again through a combination of householder dissatisfaction and a resultant new technology. Granite-cobbled streets were noisy, dusty and disagreeable for drivers of the new horseless carriages. The answer was tarmac. Silent, easy to apply and much cheaper than granite cobbles. Sadly, for Guernsey, the UK based Mowlem company who had nurtured the local stone exporting industry, found no need to develop their tarmac business from the island. Quarrying suffered the triple blow of consumer irritation, new technology and a lack of a local champion.

How lucky was Guernsey's fifth brand! Just as shipbuilding was in its death-throes, and quarrying had passed its peak; a little red fruit accessed local skills. Granite foundation walls topped with upside-down wooden boat frames and fitted with glass panes, facilitated the birth of the Guernsey Tom. In local greenhouses it began its climb to market greatness. Bit-by-bit the

8: And The Moral Of This Story Is?

English consumer grew used to the idea of a salad or sandwich with tomatoes. And every British household came to know the Guernsey Tom.

A truly great consumer brand. But, having built what marketers call brand awareness over a period of 50 years (1905–1955), there followed a 22-year period of flat sales from 1956 to 1978. The island's horticulturalists were lulled into a false sense of security and then quite abruptly the industry collapsed following a ten-year free-fall. It finally gave up completely in 1999. We have already covered in detail the reasons for the fall but to summarise, we can blame the States for lack of industry leadership, the Dutch for their incredible business foresight and cheap gas, the UK government for joining the EU and unleashing the availability of Iberian tomatoes, the local growers for their unwillingness to modernise, the finance industry for providing a better source of employment, and, finally, the UK consumers for wanting cheap tomatoes.

Quietly in the background, since the early 19th century was Guernsey's sixth brand, tourism. It really took off after World War 2, as paid holidays became universally available. Guernsey's beaches, sunshine and accessibility attracted thousands to the island. Guest houses alongside greenhouses provided a good income for many of the island's population.

Happy days. But you know what's coming! Our British consumers wanted more sunshine, more entertainment and cheaper travel. All available on the coast of Spain. The Guernsey tourist brand lost its appeal and the island failed to adapt to new circumstances, failed to find a new consumer need and failed to quickly reinvent its offer.

It still survives, providing a ready-made infrastructure of transport links, restaurants and hotels for the clients of the emerging finance industry. And today it's not as dominant as it once was, but now, as part service provider for the offshore industry and part long-weekend resort for UK baby boomers.

And so, we come to the latest Guernsey brand – the offshore finance industry. From 1962, like all the previous Guernsey brands, it steadily built reputation and brand awareness, reaching a peak around 2005, in terms of percentage of the island's GDP. Since then, the signs are that it is declining, impacted by global competition, government intervention and a general bad public image, as countries are keen to get their hands on more tax revenue from corporations.

Will financial services last longer than the 200-plus years of stocking exports, the 150 years of quarrying, the 100 years of privateering/smuggling/entrepôt, the 94 years of tomato growing, the 82 years of shipbuilding, and the 78 years of tourism? So far, offshore finance has been around for just over 60 years. And it has learnt from the previous brands by listening to its consumers and innovating many new services. Will this be enough to keep the finance brand alive? There are the troubling signs of the decline in bank numbers. If the previous six Guernsey brands are anything to go by, then if the finance industry does decline, it will happen quite quickly.

What has all this taught us? More importantly, what can it teach Guernsey's current income earner? First: don't trust governments. They can sometimes help but mostly they are damaging to a tiny entity like Guernsey. Second: the sea that surrounds the island can be an ally but also an enemy. It provided fast, cheap accessibility in the era of dreadful roads, but became a barrier once roads and rail connections made distant challengers more accessible. Third: don't trust outside partners whose economic interests are not influenced by island patriotism. These outside forces messed up quarrying, have not helped tourism and seem to be weakening the finance industry. Fourth: don't believe a particular business specialisation

8: And The Moral Of This Story Is?

will protect the island's economy forever. Don't try to preserve a dying industry beyond sensible book balancing. Look outward for a replacement, not inward with shoring-up actions.

Finally, and without doubt the most important lesson from the histories of the seven brands described in this book, don't take your eye off the consumer. Listen attentively to their changing needs, respond to them, no matter how painful it might be. The chances are that Guernsey's future will come from a consumer demand that could be miles away from today's finance industry. It could be helped by the sea around the island or other natural resources. It could perhaps benefit from a piece of government legislation. Maybe something new could come from an entrepreneur spotting a beneficial element in the island's makeup. The next big Guernsey brand could already be on the island today – a little start-up green shoot waiting to become our eighth Guernsey brand.

One thing is for sure; the island of Guernsey and its people have shown extraordinary resilience in the past 500 years. They have shown amazing resourcefulness. And they have shown an unquenchable independence of spirit. It would be a very brave person to bet against the Bailiwick not reinventing itself yet again.

Timeline

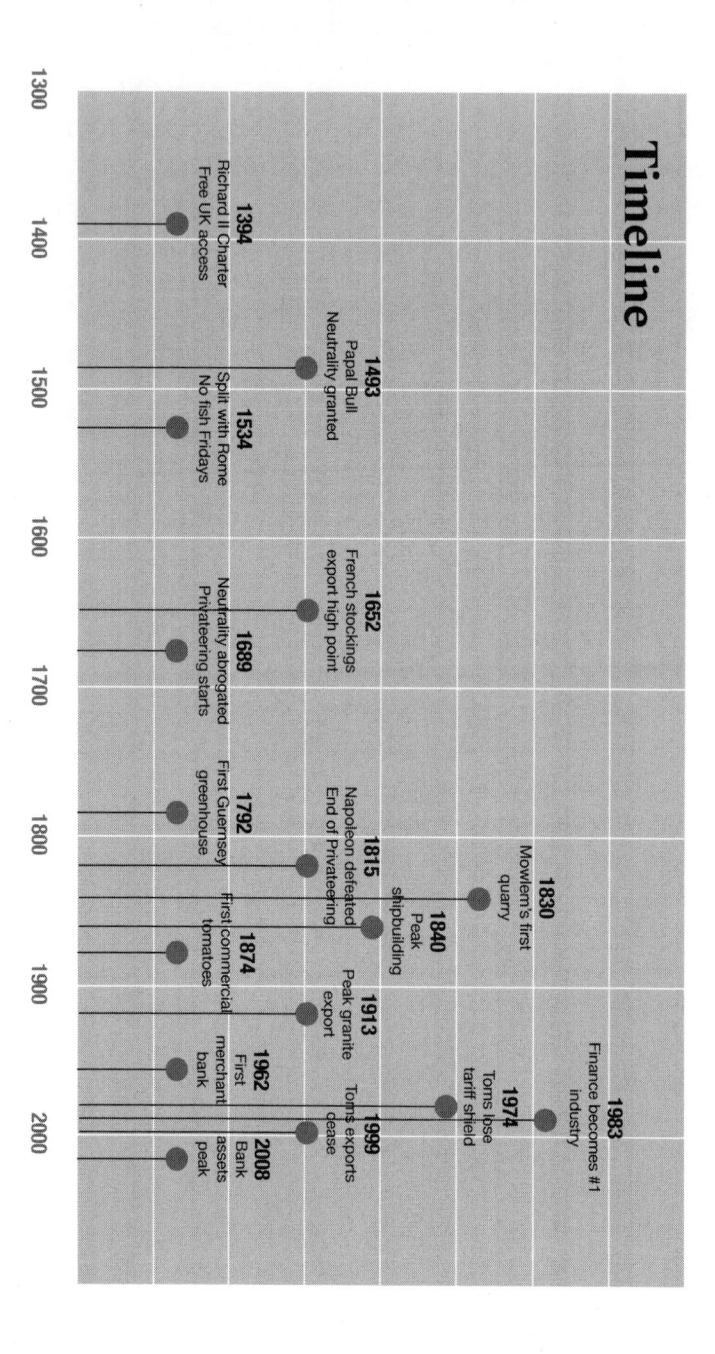

- **1394** Richard II Charter — Free UK access
- **1493** Papal Bull — Neutrality granted
- **1534** Split with Rome — No fish Fridays
- **1652** French stockings export high point
- **1689** Neutrality abrogated — Privateering starts
- **1792** First Guernsey greenhouse
- **1815** Napoleon defeated — End of Privateering
- **1830** Mowlem's first quarry
- **1840** Peak shipbuilding
- **1874** First commercial tomatoes
- **1913** Peak granite export
- **1962** First merchant bank
- **1974** Toms lose tariff shield
- **1983** Finance becomes #1 industry
- **1999** Toms exports cease
- **2008** Bank assets peak

Appendix: Data Sources for Graphs

Fig 1: Population (page 7).
1881–1899: *Billets d'Etat,* 1900.
Dury (1948).
Crossan (2007).
States of Guernsey website (gov.gg).

Fig 2: Ships Built (page 59).
Sharp (1970).

Fig 3: Stone Exports (page 68).
1828/1837/1852: Fenn & Yeoman (2008).
1855: Jamieson (1986).
1893/1895/1896: GCC AGM Reports (IAG).
1972/1914: Robinson (1977).
Girard (1986).
Girard (1982).
Crossan (2007).

Fig 4: Tomato Exports (page 96).
Before 1986: GTMB (IAG).
After 1987: GGGA (IAG).
1894–2015: GGA Minute Books (IAG).
1896–2014: GGA Annual Reports and Yearbooks (IAG).

Fig 5: Tourist Arrivals (page 132).

    1958/1970: *Billet d'Etat*, September 1971.
    1991–2019: *Guernsey Facts & Figures*, States of Guernsey (gov.gg).
    1946–1967: Girard (1967) .
    GCC *Contact* magazine (IAG).
    Uttley (1966).

Fig 6: Number of Banks (page 191).

    Press Directories, 1962–1970 (Priaulx Library).
    Telephone Directories, 1970–2022 (Priaulx Library).
    GFSC, 1990–2020.

Fig 7: Bank Deposits (page 191).

    'Bank Deposits', https://www.gfsc.gg/industry-sectors/banking/statistics (last accessed 11 Feb 2024).
    Figures reworked at 2023 values using the Bank of England inflation calculator (https://www.bankofengland.co.uk/monetary-policy/inflation/inflation-calculator).

Abbreviations

GCC	Guernsey Chamber of Commerce
GFSC	Guernsey Financial Services Commission
GGA	Guernsey Growers Association
GTMB	Guernsey Tomato Marketing Board
IAG	Island Archives, Guernsey
TSG	Transactions of La Société Guernesiaise
RGS	The Review of the Guernsey Society

Bibliography

Printed Sources

Anon, 'Guernsey, its present state and future prospects: Society, 1846', *Dublin University Magazine* (1846).

Acton, Eliza, *Modern Cooking for Private Families* (1845).

Addison, Timothy, 'Shooting Blanks: the War on Tax Havens' *Indiana Journal of Global Legal Studies* 16:2 (2009)

Allende, Sam, *Be More Pirate* (2018).

Ansted, DT & RG Latham, *The Channel Islands* (1862).

Mrs Beeton's Book of Household Management (1861).

Bailey, PF, 'Modernisation & Early Growing from an English Grower's Point of View', *GGA Review & Yearbook* (1959)

Berkers, E. and F. W. Geels. 'System innovation through stepwise reconfiguration: the case of technological transitions in Dutch greenhouse horticulture (1930–1980)', *Technology Analysis and Strategic Management* No.23, March 2011.

Berry, William, *The History of the Island of Guernsey* (1815).

Bescoby, AC, *Modern Horticulture* (1904).

Best, Michael, *A Family Business* (2006).

Birch, Rex, 'Guernsey Tourism – is it worth its place?', *RGS* Summer 1989.

Bishop, A, *Guernsey Chamber of Commerce* (1869).

Bouvatier, Capelle-Blancard, Delatte, 'April 2017 Meeting of the National Tax Association', *European Banks and Tax Havens*, vol. 110 (2017).

Carey Olsen, *Investment Funds: why choose Guernsey?*, 30 Jan 2019.

Clutterbuck, Lady Maria aka Mrs Charles Dickens, *What Shall We Have for Dinner?* (1852).

Coysh, Victor, 'The Guernsey Shipbuilding Industry, *TSG* XV:3 (1952).

CR, 'Guernsey', *The Guernsey Magazine* (April 1893).

Craig, Elizabeth, *Family Cookery* (1935).

Crossan, Rose-Marie, *Guernsey 1814–1914: Migration and Modernisation* (2007).

Crossan, Rose-Marie, *Poverty and Welfare in Guernsey 1560–2015* (2015).

Daly, Gavin, 'English Smugglers, the Channel and the Napoleonic Wars, 1800–1814', *Journal of British Studies* (Jan 2007).

David, Elizabeth, *French Provincial Cooking* (1960).

De la Rue, D, *The Guernsey Free Churchman* (December 1926).

Dempster, JH, 'The Future for Guernsey Horticulture', *GTMB* (March 1981).

Dods, Matilda Lees, *Handbook of Practical Cookery* (1906).

Doshi, Vidhi, 'The small Dutch town that wants to shape the future of your food', *The Guardian*, 5 March 2020.

Duncan, Jonathan, *The History of Guernsey : with occasional notices of Jersey, Alderney, and Sark* (1841).

Dury, GH, 'The Population of Guernsey', *Geography*, 33:2 (June 1948).

Dury, GH, 'Land use statistics in Guernsey in the late 18th century', *Transactions of La Société Guernesiaise*, XV:4 (1953).

Estabrook, Barry, 'On the Tomato Trail: In Search of Ancestral Roots', *Gastronomica Magazine* (May 2010).

Evans, D, 'President's Report', *Guernsey Chamber of Commerce News*, No.10 (December 1978).

Falla, RJ, *Some notes on quarrying in Guernsey* (1998).

Fenn, RWD & AB Yeoman, *Quarrying in Guernsey, Alderney and Herm* (2008).

Foote, Stephen, 'The 1948 Channel Islands Liberation Postage Stamps and the Revival of the Tourist Industry', *RGS* (2016).

Francatelli, Charles Elmé, *The Modern Cook: A Practical Guide to the Culinary Art* (1845).

Gallienne, Tony, *Guernsey in the 21st Century* (2007).

Gardiner, V, 'The same but different – 19th century tourism in the Channel Islands and the visit of Sir David Wedderbern, 1873' *TSG* XXIV:1 (1996).

Gerard, John, *The Herball or Generall Historie of plantes* (1597).

Girard, Peter, 'The Guernsey Grape Industry' *TSG* XV:2 (1951).

Girard, Peter, 'Geographic aspects of Tourism in Guernsey', *TSG* (1967).

Girard, Peter, *Peter Girard's Guernsey* (1986).

Gourvish, TR, *British Rail Ways 1948–1973* (1986).

Hampton, Mark, *The Offshore Interface: Tax havens in the Global Economy* (1996).

Hampton & Christensen, 'Competing Industries in Islands', *Annals of Tourism Research*, 34:4 (2007).

Harris, GF, *Granite and Our Granite Industries* (1888).

Hebous, Shakik, 'Money at the docks of Tax Havens', *Public Finance Analysis* 70:3 (February 2014).

Heylyn, Peter, *A Full Relation of Two Journeys* (1656).

Hill & Co, *Historical Directory of the Channel Islands* (1874).

Hill, Thomas, *The Gardeners Labyrinth* (1577).

Hinton, WL, 'Outlook for Horticulture', *Occasional papers*, University of Cambridge. School of Agriculture (June 1968).

Hocart. Richard, 'The Journal of C. Trumbull', *TSG* XXI:4 (1985).

Hocart, Richard, 'Monseiur de St. George: Jean Guille (1712-1778), *TSG* XXVI:5 (2010).

Hocart, Richard, *The Country People of Guernsey and their Agriculture 1640–1840* (2016).

House, John, *Renoir 1841–1919*, Guernsey Museum (1990).

Howard, Terry, 'The Bouet, Backache and Brouards', GGA (2009).

Inglis, Henry D, *The Channel Islands* (1834).

Jacob, John, *Annals of some of the British Norman Isles* (1830).

Jamieson, AG (ed.), *A People of the Sea: A Maritime History of the Channel Islands* (1986).

Jeffery, S, *Pebbles, Post & Purbeck Paving – a study of early 18th century street paving in London* (1988), published by: The Association for Studies in the Conservation of Historic Buildings.

Johns, RA & CM Le Marchant, *Finance Centres: British Isle Offshore Development Since 1979* (1993).

Lee, Marshall M, *Winning with People: the First 40 years of Tektronix* (1986).

Lewer, David, *John Mowlem's Swanage Diary 1845–1851* (1990).

Lewis, Samuel, *A Topographical Dictionary of England* (1833).

Loudon, John Claudius, *Encyclopaedia of Gardening* (1822).

Marr, L James, *A History of the Bailiwick of Guernsey* (1982).

Mathew, WM, *The Secret History of Guernsey Marmalade: James Keiller & Son Offshore, 1857–1879* (1998).

McAdam, J, *A Practical Essay on the Scientific Repair & Preservation of Public Roads* (March 1819), Open Library.

Miles, John (ed), *A Kitchen Goes to War* (1940).

Monod, Paul, 'Dangerous Merchandise: Smuggling, Jacobitism, and Commercial Culture in Southeast England, 1690–1760', *Journal of British Studies*, 30:2 (Apr 1991).

Muldrew, Craig, 'Th'ancient Distaff and 'Whirling Spindle': measuring the contribution of spinning to household earnings and the national economy in England 1550–1770', *Economic History Review* 65:2 (2012).

Nye, John V, *War, Wine & Taxes* (2007).

Ogier, Darryl, *Reformation & Society in Guernsey* (1996).

Palan, Ronen, *The Spider's Web* (film), released 2017.

Palan, Ronen, 'Tax Havens and the Commercialisation of State Sovereignty', *International Organisation*, 56:1, Winter 2002.

Phillipson, David, *Smuggling: a history* (1973).

Priaulx, TF and R De Saumarez, 'The Guernsey Stocking Trade', *TSG* XVII:2(1961).

Quayle, Thomas, *General View of the Agriculture and present state of the Islands on the Coast of Normandy* (1815).

Raban, Peter, 'War & Trade in the mid-18th century', *TSG* XXII:1 (1986).

Raistrick, A, 'Spinning Wheels from the Channel Islands', *Spinning Wheel Sleuth, issue 28,* April 2000.

Renouf, John, 'Geological excursion guide 1: Jersey and Guernsey, Channel Islands', *Geology Today* (May/June 1985).

Richards, J & JM Mackenzie, *The Railway Station: A Social History*, (1988)

Richardson, David, 'Chasing the Artful Dodger', *Australia Quarterly*, Oct-Dec 2019.

Robinson, WS, *Guernsey* (1977).

Schenk, Catherine, 'The Origins of the Eurodollar Market 1955–1963', *Explorations in Economic History*, vol. 35 (1998), pp. 221–238.

Sharp, EW, 'The Shipbuilders of Guernsey', *TSG* XVIII:5 (1970).

Shaxson, Nicolas, *Treasure Islands: Tax Havens and the Men who Stole the World* (2012).

Shewell-Cooper, Wilfred, *The Book of the Tomato* (1948).

Smith, Barry, *The Island* (2017).

Smith, Delia, *Complete Illustrated Cooking Course* (1989).

Stevens Cox, Gregory, *St Peter Port 1680–1830: the History of an International Entrepôt* (1999).

Stott, Ronnie, 'When tomatoes were blamed for witchcraft and werewolves', AtlasObscura, https://www.atlasobscura.com/articles/when-tomatoes-were-blamed-for-witchcraft-and-werewolves (last accessed 11 Feb 2024).

Thirsk, Joan, 'The Fantastical Folly of Fashion: The English Stocking Knitting Industry 1500–1700', in *Textile History and Economic History: Essays in Honour of Julia de Lacy Mann*, ed. NB Harte and KG Ponting (Manchester University Press, 1973).

Thomson, R, 'Pebbles, Pots and Bangs' in *Guernsey Connections* ed. Heather Sebire (1998).

Tupper, FB, 'Commerce of Guernsey', *The Guernsey & Jersey Magazine* (December 1837).

Tupper, FB, *The history of Guernsey and its bailiwick; with occasional notices of Jersey* (1854).

Uttley, John, *The Story of the Channel Islands* (1966).

Vermeulen, S, 'Tourism needs more support and fewer gestures from the States', *Contact* magazine (GCC, May 2002).

Wall, ET, 'Guernsey Horticulture – where next?', *Guernsey Growers Association Yearbook* (1973).

Wheadon, EA, 'The History and Cultivation of the Tomato in Guernsey', *GGA Yearbook* (1937).

Periodicals

Billet d'Etats, States of Guernsey.

Contact magazine, GCC.

Gentleman's Magazine.

Guernsey Facts and Figures, States of Guernsey.

Morning Chronicle.

States Economic Overview, States of Guernsey.

The Guernsey & Jersey Magazine.

The Star, Guernsey.

United Service Magazine.

Websites

'Five Ways to Compute the Relative Value of a UK Pound Amount, 1270 to present', MeasuringWorth, 2024, www.measuringworth.com/ukcompare/ (last accessed 11 Feb 2024).

'Focus: How healthy is Guernsey's Finance Industry?', *Bailiwick Express*, 16 June 2023, https://gsy.bailiwickexpress.com/gsy/news/focus-how-healthy-guernseys-finance-industry/(last accessed 11 Feb 2024).

'Guernsey Letters of Marque', *Donkipedia*, www.theislandwiki.org/index.php/Guernsey_Letters_of_Marque (last accessed 11 Feb 2024).

'Guernsey & the Great Exhibition, 1851', *Guernsey Museum*, https://museums.gov.gg/CHttpHandler.ashx?id=76911&p=0 (last accessed 11 Feb 2024).

'Interview with Dave Spinks', *TekTalk* (Tektronix newsletter) 7 Aug 2017, Vintagetek.org (last accessed 11 Feb 2024).

'London's Road Surfaces and Pavements', *Greater London Industrial Archaeology Society*, http://www.glias.org.uk/news/231news.html#C (last accessed 11 Feb 2024).

'Memories of Peter Perchard', *Priaulx Library*, https://www.priaulxlibrary.co.uk/articles/article/memories-peter-perchard (last accessed 11 Feb 2024).

'Vehicle numbers in Guernsey continue to rise', *BBC News*, 7 September 2010, https://www.bbc.co.uk/news/world-europe-guernsey-11211598, (last accessed 11 Feb 2024).

Globalbanks.com (last accessed 11 Feb 2024).

Kenya-Advisor.com (last accessed 11 Feb 2024).

MaraRiley.net (last accessed 11 Feb 2024).

BIBLIOGRAPHY

Institute of Civil Engineers Library, London

John Mowlem and Co Ltd, Directors' Minute Books.

Island Archives, Guernsey

Falla, RJ, 'Some Notes on Quarrying in Guernsey' (1998).
Gallienne, WT, 'A History of Quarrying in Guernsey', a talk to members of La Société Guernesiaise, 12 November 1988.
GCC Archives.
GGA Yearbooks.
GTMB Minute Books.

London Metropolitan Archives

Records of John Mowlem & Company Ltd and subsidiary companies (ACC/2809).

Unpublished Sources

Doyle, Andrew, 'Analysis of glasshouse location in Guernsey', University of Southampton thesis (unpublished).

Endnotes

Introduction
1. Mathew (1998).

1: An Unexpected Start
1. Stevens Cox (1999).
2. Crossan (2015).
3. Dury (1953).
4. Thirsk (1973).
5. Raistrick (2000).
6. Muldrew (2012).
7. Priaulx & De Saumarez (1961).
8. Priaulx & De Saumarez (1961).
9. Dury (1948).
10. MaraRiley.net.
11. Heylyn (1656).
12. Hocart (2016).
13. Heylyn (1656), quoted in Ogier (1996).
14. Hocart (1985).
15. The Earl of Warwick quoted in Priaulx & de Saumarez (1961).
16. Hocart (2016).
17. Thirsk (1973).
18. De Saumarez letters of the 1670s quoted in Priaulx & De Saumarez, (1961).
19. William Le Marchant (1684), quoted in Priaulx & De Saumarez (1961).
20. Hocart (2016).
21. William Le Marchant (1771), quoted in Stevens Cox (1999).
22. Tupper (1837), quoting Jacobs (1830).

2: The Slightly Naughty Century
1. 'Entrepôt', *Wikipedia*, https://en.wikipedia.org/wiki/Entrepôt (last accessed 11 Feb 2024).
2. Stevens Cox (1999).

3 *Morning Chronicle* (1788).
4 Hocart (2010).
5 Jamieson (1986).
6 Raban (1986).
7 Jamieson (1986).
8 'Guernsey Letters of Marque', *Donkipedia*, www.theislandwiki.org/index.php/Guernsey_Letters_of_Marque (last accessed 11 Feb 2024).
9 as above.
10 'Cutter (boat), *Wikipedia*, https://en.wikipedia.org/wiki/Cutter_(boat), (last accessed 11 Feb 2024).
11 'Memories of Peter Perchard', Priaulx Library website, https://www.priaulxlibrary.co.uk/articles/article/memories-peter-perchard.
12 *Gentleman's Magazine* vol. 18 (1748), Priaulx Library.
13 Edmund Burke quoted in Marr (1982).
14 Hocart (2016).
15 Allende (2018).
16 Importation Act (1744).
17 Nye (2007).
18 Monod (1991).
19 Girard (1986).
20 The Treasury (1807) quoted in Daly (2007).
21 Phillipson (1973).
22 Berry (1815).
23 Monod (1991), qv
24 Collector of Customs (1804), quoted in Daly (2007), qv
25 Thomas Turner quoted in Monod (1991).

3: The Industry That Left No Trace

1 Berry (1815).
2 Tupper (1854).
3 Quoted in Jamieson (1986).
4 Berry (1815).
5 Sharp (1970).
6 Victor Coysh (1952).
7 Jacob (1830).
8 Jamieson (1986).

9 Sharp (1970).
10 Tupper (1837).
11 Coysh (1952).
12 D. De la Rue in *The Guernsey Free Churchman* (December 1926).
13 Sharp (1970).
14 Sharp (1970).
15 Tupper (December 1837).
16 Victor Hugo quoted in Jamieson (1986).
17 'List of ships built in Guernsey', *Donkipedia*, https://theislandwiki.org/index.php/List_of_Ships_built_in_Guernsey (last accessed 11 Feb 2024).
18 *The Star*, Guernsey (24 Dec 1828).

4: Guernsey Rocks

1 Conversation with Martin Smith Reader in Geology at the University of Brighton.
2 Renouf (1985).
3 Marr (1982).
4 Fenn & Yeoman (2008).
5 Best (2006).
6 Jeffery (1988).
7 Jeffrey (1988).
8 Hocart (2016).
9 Thomson (1998).
10 Thomson (1998).
11 Tupper (1837).
12 Lewis (1833).
13 McAdam (1821).
14 McAdam (1819).
15 Fenn & Yeoman (2008).
16 Robinson (1977).
17 'John Mowlem', *Wikipedia*, https://en.wikipedia.org/wiki/John_Mowlem (last accessed 11 Feb 2024).
18 Lewer (1990).
19 Lewer (1990).
20 Lewer (1990).

ENDNOTES

21 Gallienne (1988) IA.
22 'London's Road Surfaces and Pavements', *Greater London Industrial Archaeology Society*, http://www.glias.org.uk/news/231news.html#C (last accessed 11 Feb 2024).
23 RJ Falla, 'Some Notes on Quarrying in Guernsey' (1998) IA.
24 'Guernsey & the Great Exhibition, 1851', https://museums.gov.gg/CHttpHandler.ashx?id=76911&p=0, last accessed 11 Feb 2024.
25 'Guernsey Chamber of Commerce AGM', *The Star*, 12 March 1885.
26 'Guernsey Chamber of Commerce AGM', *The Star*, 15 March 1888.
27 Harris (1888).
28 'Guernsey Chamber of Commerce AGM', *The Star*, 12 March 1885.
29 'Guernsey Chamber of Commerce AGM', *The Star*, 15 March 1888.
30 Guernsey Chamber of Commerce AGM', *The Star*, 27 February 1883.
31 Mowlem Properties, LMA ACC/2809.
32 Mowlem, Minute Book, 10 November 1913.
33 Mowlem, Minute Book, 10 November 1913.
34 Mowlem, Minute Book, 11 September 1918.
35 Mowlem, Minute Book, 17 June 1926.
36 Mowlem, Minute Book, 17 January 1928.
37 Mowlem, Minute Book, AGM 1930.
38 Fenn & Yeoman (2008).

5: Who Killed the Guernsey Tom?

1 Gerard (1597).
2 Ronnie Stott, 'When tomatoes were blamed for witchcraft and werewolves', AtlasObscura, https://www.atlasobscura.com/articles/when-tomatoes-were-blamed-for-witchcraft-and-werewolves (last accessed 11 Feb 2024).
3 'Tomato', *Wikipedia*, https://en.wikipedia.org/wiki/Tomato, last accessed 11 Feb 2024.
4 Loudon (1822).
5 Clutterbuck (1852)
6 Dury (1953).
7 Dury (1953).
8 Quayle (1815).
9 Inglis (1834).

10 Hill (1874).
11 Girard (1951).
12 Jacob (1830).
13 Girard (1951).
14 Jacob (1830).
15 Wheadon (1937).
16 Girard (1986).
17 CR (April 1893).
18 Doyle (unpublished).
19 Guernsey Chamber of Commerce AGM, *The Star*, 25 April 1889.
20 Estabrook (2010).
21 'A Growth Industry', *Guernsey Press*, 26 July 2022.
22 *GGA Review* (January 1955).
23 Shewell-Cooper (1948).
24 Interview carried out as part of 'Analysis of glasshouse location in Guernsey', unpublished University of Southampton thesis by A. Doyle.
25 Various volumes of the *Billet d'Etat*, 1917–1927.
26 Hinton (1968).
27 'A Growth Industry', *Guernsey Press*, 26 July 2022.
28 Wall (1973).
29 Robinson (1977).
30 *GGA Annual Report & Yearbook* (1965).
31 *GGA Annual Report & Yearbook* (1969).
32 Hinton (1968).
33 *GGA Annual Report & Yearbook* (1968).
34 Howard (2009).
35 *GGA Annual Report & Yearbook* (1985).
36 *Billets d'Etat*, Vol LVII (1971).
37 *Billets d'Etat*, Vol LVII (1971).
38 *Billets d'Etat*, Vol LVII (1971).
39 Dempster (1981).
40 Dempster (1981).
41 *GGA Review & Yearbook* (1981).
42 *Billets d'Etat*, Vol LX (1974).
43 *Billets d'Etat*, Vol LX (1974).

Endnotes

44 *GGA Review & Yearbook* (1981).
45 Bailey (1959).
46 *GGA Review & Yearbook* (1960).
47 Vidhi Doshi, 'The small Dutch town that wants to shape the future of your food', *The Guardian*, 5 March 2020, https://www.theguardian.com/world/2020/mar/05/how-a-small-dutch-town-is-shaping-the-future-of-your-food-wageningen-netherlands (last accessed 11 Feb 2024).
48 Berkers & Geels (2011).
49 *GGA Review & Yearbook* (1965).
50 *GGA Review & Yearbook* (1989).
51 RG Kimber in *GGA Annual Report and Yearbook* (1982).
52 RG Kimber in *GGA Annual Report and Yearbook* (1982).
53 Beeton (1861).
54 *GGA Annual Report and Yearbook* (1986).
55 *GTMB 29th Annual Report* (1981).
56 *GGA Annual Report and Yearbook* (1983).
57 GTMB Memo dated 10 October 1986, IAG.
58 *GGA Annual Report and Yearbook* (1999).
59 *GGA Annual Report and Yearbook* (1998).

6: Buckets, Spades & Windbreaks

1 Smith (2017).
2 'A Run to the Channel Islands', *United Service Magazine*, Vol 26 (1838).
3 Google Ngrams, http://books.google.com/ngrams (last accessed 11 Feb 2023).
4 Carré, SD, 'Tourism & the Sark Community' *TSG* XXII:4 (1989).
5 Bishop (1869).
6 Ansted & Latham (1862).
7 *The Comet*, May 1838)
8 Duncan (1841).
9 Gardiner (1996).
10 Gardiner (1996).
11 Hills (1874).
12 House (1990).
13 'Guernsey, its present state and future prospects: Society, 1846', *Dublin*

University Magazine (1846).
14. 'A Run to the Channel Islands', *United Service Magazine,* Vol 26 (1838).
15. 'Guernsey, its present state and future prospects: Society, 1846', *Dublin University Magazine* (1846).
16. Bishop (1869).
17. GCC AGM (1876) IA.
18. Uttley (1966).
19. Gardiner (1996).
20. Uttley (1966).
21. Girard (1967).
22. Marr (1982).
23. Girard (1967).
24. Girard (1967).
25. Foote (2016).
26. *Guernsey Facts and Figures*, States of Guernsey (1989).
27. Guernsey Met Office Annual Reports, http://www.metoffice.gov.gg/annualstats.html(last accessed 11 Feb 2024).
28. 'Victor Hugo & Guernsey: Lost Things: La Marcherie', Priaulx Library website, https://www.priaulxlibrary.co.uk/articles/article/victor-hugo-and-guernsey-lost-things-la-marcherie (last accessed 11 Feb 2024).
29. Richards & Mackenzie (1988)
30. Gourvish (1986).
31. S. Vermeulen, 'Tourism needs more support and fewer gestures from the States', *Contact* magazine (GCC, May 2002).
32. Guernsey Airport website, airport.gg.
33. Island Development Committee Outline Plan, *Billet d'Etat* LIII p.385 (1967).
34. Billets d'Etat, 1967 (as above).
35. 'Guernsey Travel Survey', *Billet d'Etat* LVII p.265 (1971).
36. 'The Future Development of Tourism', *Billet d'Etat* LVIII p.703 (1972).
37. 'Guernsey Travel Survey', *Billet d'Etat* LVII p.265 (1971).
38. D. Evans, 'President's Report', *GCC News*, No 10 (December 1978).
39. '1992 Policy Planning, Economic & Financial Report', *Billet d'Etat* LXXVIII p.739 (1992).
40. 'Economic Appraisal of the Island', *Billet d'Etat* LXXIII p.950 (1987).

Endnotes

41 'Tourist Board Tourism Survey 1983', *Billet d'Etat* LXX p.299 (1984).
42 Birch (1989).
43 'Economic Appraisal of the Island', *Billet d'Etat* LXXIII p.950 (1987).
44 *Contact* magazine, GCC, July 1989.
45 'Guernsey Travel Survey', *Billet d'Etat* LVII p.265 (1971).
46 '1983 Tourism Survey', *Billet d'Etat* LXX p.299 (1984).
47 'Interview with Dave Spinks', *TekTalk* (Tektronix newsletter) 7 Aug 2017, Vintagetek.org (last accessed 11 Feb 2024).
48 'Vehicle numbers in Guernsey continue to rise', *BBC News*, 7 September 2010, https://www.bbc.co.uk/news/world-europe-guernsey-11211598, (last accessed 11 Feb 2024).
49 'List of countries and territories by motor vehicles per capita', *Wikipedia*, https://en.wikipedia.org/wiki/List_of_countries_and_territories_by_motor_vehicles_per_capita (last accessed 11 Feb 2024).
50 '1991 Policy Planning, Economic and Financial Report', *Billet d'Etat* LXXVII p.613 (1991).
51 '1991 Policy Planning, Economic and Financial Report', *Billet d'Etat* LXXVII p.613 (1991).
52 *Contact* magazine, GCC, April 1993.
53 'Policy Planning, Economic and Financial Report, 1992', *Billet d'Etat* LXXVIII p.739, (1992)
54 *Contact* magazine, GCC, April 1994.
55 'Interview with Stuart Falla', *Contact* magazine, GCC, February 1996.
56 John Gollop, 'Tourism Under the Microscope', *Contact* magazine, GCC, May 1996.
57 Rodney Brouard, 'GGA President's Prediction', *Contact* magazine, GCC, December 2000.
58 Geoff Norman, 'President's Remarks', *Contact* magazine, GCC, March 1998.
59 *Contact* magazine, GCC, June/July 2008.
60 *Contact* magazine, GCC, October 2003
61 'Interview with Tom Castledine', *Contact* magazine, GCC, December 2002.
62 Chris Elliot, *Contact* magazine, GCC, May 2008.
63 'Interview with Geoff Norman', *Contact* magazine, GCC, October

2002.
64. 'Condor Ferries Problems Putting Off Return Visitors', *Guernsey Press*, 3 August 2019.
65. 'Visitors to Guernsey spending £146m in total', BBC News, 28 February 2020 (last accessed 11 Feb 2024).
66. 'Tourism Product and Customer Experience Strategic Review', States of Guernsey website, https://www.gov.gg/article/171000/Tourism-Product-and-Customer-Experience-Strategic-Review---Full-Report (last accessed 11 Feb 2024).
67. 2010 figure from *Island Life* website, https://www.islandlife.org/guernsey.htm (last accessed 11 Feb 2024); 2017 figure from *Guernsey Harbours* website, https://harbours.gg/article/162144/2017-cruise-ship-season-has-come-to-an-end (last accessed 11 Feb 2024).

7: Offshore or Offside?

1. Hampton (1996).
2. 'Island Development Committee: Outline Plan', *Billet d'Etat* LIII p.385 (1967).
3. The history of Tektronix in Guernsey is well covered in Lee (1986).
4. Author's interview with Frank Doyle, an early employee of Tektronix.
5. *Contact* magazine, GCC, January 1990.
6. Quote from Rush & Tomkins the developers of Fort George.
7. *Making Sense of Society*, Open University, first transmission 20 March 1975.
8. *Making Sense of Society* (1975).
9. Tim Bentley, Managing Director of Royal Bank of Canada Guernsey, quoted in Hampton (1996).
10. 'Policy Planning, Economic and Financial Report, 1992', *Billet d'Etat*, LXXVIII p.739, 1992.
11. John Langlois, keynote speaker at Institute of Directors conference in 1998, quoted in the GCC *Contact* magazine.
12. Catherine Schenk, 'The Origins of the Eurodollar Market 1955–1963', *Explorations in Economic History*, vol. 35 (1998), pp. 221–238.
13. Schenk (1998).
14. Quoted in Schenk (1998).
15. Ronen Palan, *The Spider's Web* (film), released 2017.

Endnotes

16 Shaxson (2012).
17 Palan (2002).
18 'Island Development Committee: Outline Plan', *Billet d'Etat* LIII p.385 (1967).
19 Gallienne (2007).
20 Hampton & Christensen (2007).
21 Palan (2002).
22 David Hinshaw, interview with the author, July 2021.
23 Keith Corbin, Executive Chairman of Nerine International Holdings Limited, interview with the author, 2021.
24 Johns & Le Marchant (1993).
25 Hampton (1996).
26 Hampton (1996).
27 'Economic Appraisal of the Island', *Billet d'Etat* LXXIII p.950 (1987).
28 Data on banks from: Press Directories 1962–1970, Telephone Directories 1970–2022, GFSC 1990–2020.
29 Philip Marr, 'Island Economies – Productivity & Prosperity the economic imperative', GFSC speech 17 Nov 2015, https://www.gfsc.gg/sites/default/files/20151207%20-%20PJM's%20slides_4.pdf (last accessed 11 Feb 2024).
30 Carey Olsen, *Investment Funds: why choose Guernsey?*, 30 January 2019.
31 'An Overview of the Types & Uses of Guernsey Law Trusts', Carey Olsen, https://www.careyolsen.com/insights/briefings/overview-types-and-uses-guernsey-law-trusts (last accessed 11 Feb 2024).
32 *Making Sense of Society*, Open University (1975).
33 *GFSC Annual Reports*, 2012–2022.
34 *GFSC Annual Report* (2022).
35 'What is Captive Insurance and What are the Benefits?' VU Capital website, https://www.vucapital.co.uk/what-is-a-captive-insurance-and-what-are-the-benefits/ (last accessed 11 Feb 2024).
36 Hampton (1996).
37 'Leading domiciles of global captive insurance companies from 2019 to 2022, by number of companies', Statista.com, https://www.statista.com/statistics/217535/leading-global-captive-domiciles/ (last accessed 11 Feb 2024).

38 'Economic Appraisal of the Island', *Billet d'Etat* LXXIII p.950 (1987).
39 *States Economic Overview*, States of Guernsey (2020).
40 Gallienne (2007).
41 *Guernsey Press*, 4 Nov 2019.
42 Richardson (2019).
43 OECD quoted in Richardson (2019).
44 Bruno Grutner quoted in Addison (2009).
45 Hebous (2014).
46 Bouvatier, Capelle-Blancard, Delatte, 'April 2017 Meeting of the National Tax Association', *European Banks and Tax Havens*, vol. 110, pp. 1–43. JSTOR, https://www.jstor.org/stable/26794456. (2017).
47 'Guernsey finance firms confident for future, survey finds', *BBC News*, 15 March 2023, https://www.bbc.co.uk/news/world-europe-guernsey-64963827 (last accessed 11 Feb 2024).
48 'Focus: How healthy is Guernsey's Finance Industry?', *Bailiwick Express*, https://gsy.bailiwickexpress.com/gsy/news/focus-how-healthy-guernseys-finance-industry/, 16 June 2023.
49 'Royal Bank of Canada to close Guernsey offices', *ITV News*, 10 January 2023, https://www.itv.com/news/channel/2023-01-10/rbc-to-close-guernsey-office-putting-89-jobs-at-risk (last accessed 11 Feb 2024).
50 'Moneyval in Brief', Council of Europe website, https://www.coe.int/en/web/moneyval/moneyval-brief (last accessed 11 Feb 2024).

About the Author

Andrew Doyle's family has lived in Guernsey since 1963. He spent half his career in industry as a New Product Developer and the other half helping run a large London design agency. Now semi-retired, he continues to write creatively for several large multinationals. He is not great on self publicity.

Acknowledgements

First and foremost, I would like to thank both the Island Archives and the Priaulx Library, who provided me with so much of their time. What wonderful institutions they are – lucky Guernsey.

Thanks to Steve Foote of Blue Ormer for taking a chance with me. Thank you to so many individuals for their time and support: Richard Corbin, Keith Corbin, Sarah Ferbrache, Chris Griffiths, Chris Haxby, David Hinshaw, Gill Lipson, Michael Munday, Ciaran O'Connell, amongst many others.

Andrew Doyle